Of Serfs and Lords

Of Serfs and Lords

Why College Tuition is Creating a Debtor Class

Richard Kelsey

ROWMAN & LITTLEFIELD
Lanham • Boulder • New York • London

Published by Rowman & Littlefield
An imprint of The Rowman & Littlefield Publishing Group, Inc.
4501 Forbes Boulevard, Suite 200, Lanham, Maryland 20706
www.rowman.com

Unit A, Whitacre Mews, 26-34 Stannary Street, London SE11 4AB

British Library Cataloguing in Publication Information Available

Library of Congress Cataloging-in-Publication Data
Library of Congress Cataloging-in-Publication Data

Names: Kelsey, Richard, 1966- author.
Title: Of serfs and lords : why college tuition is creating a debtor class /
    Richard Kelsey.
Description: Lanham : Rowman & Littlefield, [2018] | Includes bibliographical
    references.
Identifiers: LCCN 2018021775 (print) | LCCN 2018032312 (ebook) | ISBN
    9781475837919 (electronic) | ISBN 9781475837896 | ISBN
    9781475837896 (cloth : alk. paper) | ISBN 9781475837902 (paperback : alk. paper)
Subjects: LCSH: Education, Higher—Economic aspects—United States. |
    Education, Higher—Aims and objectives—United States. | College
    costs—United States.
Classification: LCC LC67.62 (ebook) | LCC LC67.62 .K45 2018 (print) | DDC
    378.3/8—dc23
LC record available at https://lccn.loc.gov/2018021775

Printed in the United States of America

For, from, and because of the love of my wife and best friend … the incomparable Jill Braun.

Contents

College Inflation Chart

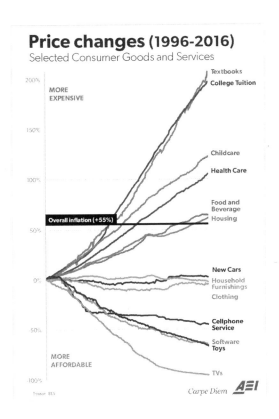

Price changes (1996-2016)
Selected Consumer Goods and Services

200%

MORE
EXPENSIVE

150%

100%

Overall inflation (+55%)

50%

0%

50%

MORE
AFFORDABLE

100%

Source: BLS

Textbooks
College Tuition

Childcare

Health Care

Food and
Beverage
Housing

New Cars
Household
Furnishings
Clothing

Cellphone
Service

Software
Toys

TVs

Carpe Diem **AEI**

Mark J. Perry, American Enterprise Institute (tweeted on August 16, 2016). https://
twitter.com/Mark_J_Perry/status/765559583066710016

Acknowledgments

I would like to acknowledge the numerous people who supported me while I wrote this book, which includes my family whom I made read it. I must, however, acknowledge one man who will never have the chance to read it, my late father. My father was World War II marine who once fought the Pentagon and won. In 1979, he picked up the cause of a stranger, a fellow marine injured in the battle of Guadalcanal. That marine earned the Medal of Honor, but through a bureaucratic error was denied the award. After numerous politicians came and went, my dad and his band of marines stood and fought for what was right, against enormous odds.

In September of 1980, President Carter awarded Anthony "Tony" Casamento his Medal of Honor. My dad was by his side in the Rose Garden that day. When Tony died, he left his medal to my father, Walter Joseph Eugene "Sarge" Kelsey.

Dad, of course, returned it to Tony's daughters.

My father never saw a wrong too big to right, and his lesson of perseverance is a lasting legacy from the greatest generation. Dad fought his way to the White House with nothing more than a high school degree and his convictions. He wanted to study law after the war, but his marriage and the arrival of seven children left that to the next generation of his children.

His inspiration is why I decided to take on the industry in which I once worked, and I am certain he has never been prouder for my doing it.

I'd also like to acknowledge the input of my test readers, whose thoughts, suggestions, and well-timed critiques kept me focused and grounded. Those readers include Nancy DeSantis, Frank Pimentel, Karen Lanpher, and David Salkin. Thank you for your time, patience, and guidance. You helped me give life to this important subject.

Preface

In this book, I attack the question that dogs most parents and education policy professionals. Why is college so darn expensive? My take is fresh, and I think it is original in many respects. Industry experts and critics alike have examined that question in great detail. The stark reality is that a particular perspective undergirds those works and analyses. Like most analyses, authors stake out a singular position and seek to defend it. We all suffer from the same weakness, which is we are predisposed to work toward a conclusion that fits our own views and interests.

I have no special powers to keep my own view, perspective, and bias in check as I look at the issues that handicap higher education. In some respects, merely being self-aware about my perspective gives me an advantage over others who look at these issues. Readers can find books and essays where professors blame administrators, administrators blame professors, university presidents blame states, governors blame university presidents, and many people blame the cheap money provided by the federal government. There is value and bias in all these works.

My book examines how many of the critiques about higher education are correct, but only in part. The great fallacy of the higher education crisis is that there exists one true explanation. Innumerable factors drive higher education costs to soar, climbing at a rate far ahead of the rate of inflation over even the most profoundly expensive services and goods. That is the point of the cover of this book. We all know college is expensive, and we have heard and read many theories about it. Few have focused on the reality that college is not only expensive, but it is getting more expensive, faster, than anything else. Fewer such books have considered all the elements, and none have offered global solutions as well as immediate, workable solutions for prospective students in the pipeline.

The theory behind this book is that several societal factors combine to create something I call "structural liberalism." That structural liberalism, with all its ingredients, drives up the cost of higher education. Another inescapable reality of structural liberalism is that our higher education system now produces a system of serfs and lords. In higher education, instead of having service providers answerable to the educational consumer, the system and incentives created inure to the benefit of the education industry, at the expense of the student. The serfs are getting deeper into debt to serve the lords and keep them in the lifestyle they prefer.

This system is broken, and reform alone is futile to combat and defeat this new feudal system where the lords profit and where they are creating a new debtor class to do so.

As we examine this reality and I push the envelope on the analysis, readers are right to ask a critical question. What makes me any more qualified to examine this issue than anyone else, and indeed, what qualifications do I have that are special to an analysis of the problem? I am a lawyer by training, so I will use an analogy that laypeople will appreciate.

In a court case, lawyers often put expert witnesses before a jury. The purpose of the expert witness is to explain a complex piece of factual evidence to the jury. The power of the witness is in several critical factors. First, the witness must be qualified before the judge and jury as an expert in the given field. In most court cases involving expert testimony, this produces a battle of experts. The first step in that battle is to introduce the witness's background and expertise to the jury so that the jury will think to itself, "Wow, this person really is an expert."

The second critical part of the expert witness duty is the strength and persuasion of the analysis he or she provides on the issues. This role of the expert is bolstered if he or she appears unbiased, and if the expert is both persuasive in his or her analysis, relatable to the jury, and credible. Only jurors can decide for themselves if the expert is credible or persuasive.

The readers of this book are my jury. I can tell you up front, I do have a bias. That bias is toward free markets, public service, lower costs, efficiency, and the traditional role of educators as mentors. That bias drives the analysis I undertake in this book and the solutions it offers.

I did not set out to write this book to defend any element or segment of the higher education industry. I set out to defend the people I identify in this book as the educational consumer. That's students and their parents. Still, as you will read in this book, even they have played a role in driving up their own costs for education. In fact, addressing the cultural expectations that give rise to their role in this mess is one easy and fast way to help students find ways to lower their own educational costs.

What are my background and qualifications to tackle this subject? If I am to be your "expert" witness, you should get the expert qualifications before you go further.

I have been involved in higher education in whole or in part for most of the last 27 years. That includes from starry-eyed student to administrator. I am not, however, merely an educationalist. Here's my background, working backward.

I served for over six years as the assistant dean for management and planning at a top-50 law school, George Mason. There, my role cut across every aspect of the law school, from budgeting, to planning, to ABA compliance, fundraising, regulations, academics, recruiting, and administrative policy. I also served prominently in public relations and marketing, appearing nationally and regionally as a legal expert and political commentator. I have appeared as a legal expert across a wide spectrum of media, from NPR to Fox Business News. I did so drawing on my unique business, academic, and technology background.

At Mason Law, I gave life to the idea of a new center for the protection of intellectual property. I conceived of the idea, wrote the budget, named the institution, helped recruit the essential faculty leaders, and I hired its executive director. That center is now one of Mason Law's most successful, and arguably the best of its centers for combing the mission of academics with hands-on teaching and scholarship. The center is called "CPIP."

In my management position, I also ultimately took over fundraising for the law school, and I had to work closely with the university advancement (development/fundraising) teams. This gave me access to the needs of the university, as well as keen insights into feedback from prospective corporate entities.

I served as a professor of law from 2007 through 2014. As I explain later in the book, technically I was an adjunct professor, teaching advanced pretrial practice and legal writing and research. Was I any good as a professor? In my last year in those duties, the graduating class elected me as the "faculty speaker" at its graduation, even though I taught the most despised course and had the duty of enforcing our honor code.

Working backward still on qualifications, I also served as an alumni board president, giving me great insight into the perspective of recent graduates as well as those who blazed the path many years before. In dealing with alumni, one also hears from and deals with the needs of the practices, agencies, and businesses that those alumni now run and what needs they want from students in the pipeline. I served on the alumni board of my law school for nearly 10 years.

I worked for one of the largest law firms in the world, and I served on the firm's committee for recruiting of new students. Indeed, I went out to schools and did some of that recruiting. Our committee laser-focused on the business and legal needs, as well as our expectation for graduates. This gave me a clear view of how businesses in the legal market viewed higher education and the entities producing prospective employees.

In my legal practice, I advised large and small companies on business and litigation decisions, many of which implicated employment issues and executive contracts. Ultimately, I became an in-house counsel and chief operating officer of a consulting company with dozens of employees across the country and globe. I later became the CEO of one of its holding companies, a forerunner in the cybersecurity industry. As CEO of a computer forensics and cybersecurity firm, I understood the needs emerging in our growing tech sector.

Even while in law school, I was selected as a student representative to our board of visitors. This role had me working side by side with the governor's appointees in formulating university policy. From that perch, I learned how a public university operated, and how it interacted with state legislators who funded it. In fact, the president of the university reported to our board, giving me an insight into university initiatives, policy making, fundraising, capital campaigns, and hiring across a then $700 million-a-year educational enterprise.

As a student, I took over and revived a dead newspaper, and I won a national award for that paper. I served as a dean's scholar, and at graduation the dean gave me the dean's service award for outstanding contributions to the school. My classmates elected me as the elected student speaker for our graduating class.

From 1990 to 1996, I was immersed as an undergraduate, both in a community college and then a state institution. Those experiences of returning to school, working during school, and trying to find value in higher education shaped many of my early thoughts on higher education.

From 1997 to the summer of 2016, I was immersed in higher education at the law school and public university level from nearly every possible angle. I brought to it diverse legal, business, public relations, writing, creative, and operational expertise. Indeed, I even brought to it fundraising and political expertise. I have viewed not only one institution, but an entire industry from nearly every possible perspective.

This book comes directly from those experiences.

RULE-BREAKERS AND RISK-TAKERS

In every industry, there are rule-breakers and risk-takers. We often hear of the powerful successes and the spectacular failure of each. However, most strong leaders in any industry, recognized or not, must at times be a rule-breaker and risk-taker. People tend to have strong feelings about rule-breakers and risk-takers. For every fan, there are critics. Sometimes there are more critics than fans. I have many critics and some fans for sure. That tells me I am doing things right—or at least as I think they are right.

This book is going to break some rules too, assuming my publisher shows a little faith in the judgment of a proven rule-breaker. When I took over my law school newspaper, the first thing the school did was cut its funding. The first thing I did was make it profitable, and hence unanswerable to those who would try to mute its voice. That's why it became such a huge success.

A former associate dean of the law school once explained, "Kelsey isn't merely the editor of the paper, he's the publisher." Many years later, the newest dean of Mason Law, before getting the job, introduced me in a meeting to a communications company by saying, "This is Kelsey, he does whatever the hell he wants." It wasn't a compliment, nor was it true, entirely. That dean eliminated my position at the law school. Sometimes risk-takers and rule-breakers don't work well together.

I have before me a "Manuscript Preparation Guide" provided by my publisher. It's excellent. Everything in it is technically correct, or certainly sound writing and publishing advice. Indeed, it's every bit as sound as the advice we give people that they ought not to be writing in the passive voice. However, truth be told, sometimes the passive voice works best. Some rules are meant to be bent, some broken, some ignored, and some … rewritten as facts dictate.

Higher education needs a revolution, not mere reform. Revolutions are not confined to rules. Indeed, a good revolution requires that we break rules and write new ones. I will do that in this book.

The rules say authors writing an academic text should do so in a third-party voice. Why? It is third-party detachment that leads to the appearance of objectivity. It is true, this book is not a personal memoir. This book also is not and cannot be a traditional academic analysis of academia. Others have drafted that tired approach. Tradition and rules do not a revolution make.

In this book, I write about the industry, but I am not merely an expert, I am a fact witness. To write completely outside of the first person would be hearsay. The power of the analysis in this book comes from objective and subjective analysis as an expert, but also from the cold reality of a first-party witness. The examples I use in the book in some places require that I put myself there—in the room—with the players and events. These antidotes don't detract from my expertise, they give evidence and insights into the conclusions and recommendations.

Great academics deal in objective analysis and provable facts. I give you that too. However, one of the great criticisms of higher education is that academics and those inside the industry live and exist in a world of theory. It's often true. Now, in this book, I combine first-person testimony with expert opinion.

When I tell you that administrators drive up education costs, I don't merely tell you how and how much, but I can give you an example of who or whom. Whatever power the literary device of third-person academic writing has, it is not more powerful in persuasion than the marriage of theory and reality. In this book, you have both expert and fact witness.

The primary thesis of this book is that our society has created something I define as "structural liberalism" that is now an iron dome over the education industry, repelling market forces, disrupting innovation, shutting out diversity of opinion, and creating barriers and obstacles to reform and efficiency. The case against this complex social and regulatory system is powerful, and it can't be told or prosecuted merely through third-party narration. The analysis must combine fact witnesses, real examples, and expert analysis.

As the book proceeds, I will introduce several terms and phrases I have used to help define and explain structural liberalism. I have included, for convenience, a glossary of these terms in the back for your reference.

Let the revolution begin.

Introduction

How to Use This Book

I examine the principal cost drivers of higher education. I do that to both answer the prescient question posed by the graph on the cover and the question that graph begs. In that respect, I write this book as a clarion call for a revolution—and not merely reform in higher education. That revolution must come from all stakeholders.

Likewise, no matter what one thinks of the answer to the question about how education became so expensive, this book is designed to help educators, legislators, regulators, students, and parents to understand this crisis in higher education costs. The primary goal is to help students and parents.

For students and parents, the book is written to help them think critically about how, if, and where to invest most wisely in a set of skills that will serve the critical economic purpose of returning an investment from tuition. To that extent, readers must disabuse themselves of the idea that they are going to college to "get an education." Life is an education. If you are to be a productive and successful member of society, education never ends.

The decision about going to college—or not going to college—must be reduced to a wise economic proposition where you pay for the tools necessary to survive and thrive in a job market. In making that investment, you must choose the right institution and degree program at the best price. In addition, in a world of limited resources and changing needs, wise investment is essential because most professions require more than one degree. Money imprudently spent on an undergraduate degree not only increases debt while limiting job opportunities, it can also result in opportunity costs—making an advanced degree too expensive.

If you are to make an informed decision about choosing to leap into the education industry as a consumer, you ought to understand that industry, how it works, why the costs are so high, and for what exactly it is that you are paying. No doubt, some will confuse this book with a hit piece on the higher education industry or simply an attack on some within it. That is not at all the purpose or intent of the book. Make no mistake, the industry needs revolution, though it can start merely with reform. Likewise, society needs to change its thinking about higher education, as it is the key component that helped to create the institutions and structure that has perverted higher education.

The problem in higher education is us.

Don't lose sight of that principal fact. Whether it is a state school, community college, or private institution, the interplay between state policies, federal lending, private loans, parental and societal expectations, and the political and profit interests of the institutions themselves is all a part of a complex educational web that has quite literally made higher education nearly unaffordable.

Society has made higher education expensive at best, and a bad investment at worst. The book examines that reality and it identifies how we have collectively built a system based on "structural liberalism" that has become self-serving, rather than consumer-serving.

The book is designed to be a series of questions. Law professors pose questions and then answer questions with more questions. This method forces students to think critically, and it stimulates analysis. The essence of education is the idea that we question nearly everything, and then we work to find verifiable or reliable answers to those questions.

Higher education is served best when it incubates thinking, giving birth to reason over emotion. Rarely is it useful, as we see today, for reason to be displaced by evoking or encouraging feelings or emotions. For that reason, the chapters start off with a big question, which then leads to more questions. Through the book, we drive together toward answers and reasonable conclusions.

You may not require the answer to every question in this book to make the right choice about choosing to invest in college—or not. In fact, to the extent that someone else wants to fully fund your "education" and is willing to do so without regard to the cost or value, many of these questions and critiques won't apply to you. Maybe you should give the book to them instead.

If you are thinking about going to college, however, and in so thinking you know that you will bear a great majority of the cost of that investment, then this book seeks to drive you to the right set of choices through examination of the current state of higher education. Getting an education, after all, is not about telling you what to think, it's about helping you to learn how to think critically.

The book uses real examples and analysis to reach conclusions. That is critical thought. The examples are anecdotal in some cases, or data driven from other sources. These examples and data are proffered to help us transparently analyze the issues. The book is designed to be relatable at every level, eschewing the need to sound professorial at every turn.

The book certainly uses and identifies data and examples that support the thesis that "structural liberalism" exists, and its components are the drivers of costs in our higher education system. Hopefully, the analogies used also will better illuminate everyone's understanding of the problems, and why and how we are moving to an educational debt crisis.

Readers may not ultimately agree with all the conclusions in the first half of this book, and some may think the perspective on tying higher education more closely to marketable skills is flawed. The book addresses that. In the end, however, the book must explain that graph on page xi. Likewise, the book must address how the industry can attack the problem, and how well-informed educational consumers can try to end-run it.

Many thinkers have tried to explain the spike in education costs, and often they focus with laser precision on a single factor, such as cheap government money. We cannot explain these higher costs by looking at just one factor. If the book is to serve the education industry and policy makers, as it should, it must lay bare why it is that textbooks and tuition are the two greatest increases in the cost of common goods and services on that chart. The answer is remarkably simple, yet profoundly complex.

Let's start with the simple, easy, elegantly American question: Why does college cost so damn much?

Part I

WHY DOES COLLEGE COST SO DAMN MUCH?

Question: Why Does College Cost So Damn Much?

Answer: Structural Liberalism … and So Much More
For Full Credit … Explain and Discuss

Chapter 1

The Cost of "Structural Liberalism" in Higher Education

Higher education costs have skyrocketed for many complex, interconnected reasons. If one had to assign a single word or phrase that best captures all the factors that drive the spiraling cost of higher education, the term that best describes this reality is "structural liberalism."

The term may be politically charged, but it is not meant to be. Indeed, the word "liberalism" is broad, vague, and subject to vast interpretations. So let's narrow the interpretation and define the term for our examination. Indeed, rather than merely using "liberalism" by itself, it is responsible and necessary to modify it to make a critical distinction between pure political perspective, and economic and societal structures.

The book examines the interplay between cultural liberalism and higher education. "Cultural liberalism" and the rise of "political" liberalism are merely elements of "structural liberalism."

In this context, "cultural liberalism" describes a political, social, and economic set of principles that disconnect market theory and efficiency from higher education as a good, service, or product. Indeed, that is why I marry the word "liberalism" to "structural." Higher education has created a web of policies, practices, regulations, and operational systems that are best described as "structural liberalism." Moreover, societal expectations and demands rooted in modern "political" liberal philosophy also play a key role in building, shaping, and supporting the structural liberalism of higher education. It is worth noting, as you will read, that "structural liberalism" is deeply in play even inside academic institutions and units thought to be politically centrist or conservative. In short, the entire higher education system works off structural liberalism.

We subject nearly nothing we do in higher education to market forces. Likewise, we don't fund loans to get an education based on market principles.

We don't evaluate loan risks based on institutions, majors, or even people. Institutions don't offer courses or majors based on their relative connection to a prospective job, and we deliver educational services in the classroom, primarily, through a workforce that is overpaid, underworked, disconnected from the consumer, and for nearly every intent or purpose, not subject to downsizing.

If capitalism is the life breath of liberty and the engine of economic prosperity and innovation, then the principles of efficiency and risk on which capitalism depends and which private industry uses to build and innovate could not be more foreign to higher education if we set out intentionally to block them from use.

Imagine trying to start a company where the government mandates that you be loaned a minimum amount of money, irrespective of credit, ability to pay it back, or the value of your business idea. Then, imagine that to build your company you must create products you can never eliminate and hire employees you can never fire. As your products become obsolete over time, imagine that you must keep selling them and forcing the consumers to pay for your unsuccessful products, even if all the consumer really wants is one of your other products.

What do you think might happen to the cost of both your products and your labor in such an example? Likewise, imagine that your labor force also cannot be told in what to invest their research, and you cannot ask them to improve their efficiency or contribute more time and hours to company priorities. How long do you think such a company could stay in business? How often do you think such a company would default on the loans it was given?

Now, imagine that to help your new company with its costs, the federal government subsidized purchases of your product to induce people to buy those products or services. In fact, imagine the government markets your product as valuable, even if all or most of it isn't, and then subsidizes your consumers through low-interest loans. Also imagine that for some reason, the state and even former consumers also contribute to your business, offsetting again some of these costs associated with creating valueless products and keeping permanent employees. That would help, right?

That might help your business pay its bills, but that doesn't help your consumers who are deeper in debt. Moreover, as the state increases regulation of your business and creates mandates related to accepting risky consumers with whom you might not normally associate or do business, it further increases your costs. Your business must find a way to cover all these costs because the structural liberalism prevents reducing many of these costs. Thus, someone must bear these expenses, right? That someone in the context of higher education is tuition payers. That someone is student loan borrowers. That someone paying all these costs is you, the educational consumer.

STRUCTURAL CAPITALISM VERSUS
STRUCTURAL LIBERALISM

In the business world, we either cut costs, innovate, or we push costs to consumers if we have no other option and if the market will bear those rising expenses. Obviously, as we can see in the graph on page xi, most market-based goods and services are at or below the annual rate of inflation. They exist in a system of efficiency; these deregulated, highly competitive industries are in structural capitalism, as opposed to structural liberalism.

Businesses are permitted, encouraged, and indeed must respond to market forces and reality. They can't keep permanent employees. They can't keep offering products the market doesn't want or value. In the business world, competition drives those choices, and the market picks winners and losers out of companies that can't or don't react smartly enough to offer useful products at a reasonable price. Higher education is not subject to market forces that compel efficiency.

Higher education doesn't really foster lower cost competition because each institution uses the same methods that drive up costs. The structure of four-year, higher education universities is nearly all the same, irrespective of which type of institution you attend. Certainly, if you go to a state school rather than a private school, you pay less tuition more often than not.

Moreover, you could start your educational career at a community college, where the education costs are much lower still. The structural issues that drive up prices in state and private schools, however, remain the same. They rely on tuition, subsidized by cheap, low-interest federal loans. They each use tenure as a mechanism to attract high-value instructors.

The practical effect of tenure is to keep a highly compensated, well-trained workforce. The reality is that such a workforce is not optimally productive, and while tenured professors often can and do jump ship for a better offer to an institution that gives them more of what they want, institutions can't eliminate the tenured professors it has if those professors give universities less than they hoped. Universities simply can't effectively cut costs because their greatest cost is in their tenured faculty and its growing administrative staff.

For that reason, competition is often not on price in higher education, but rather value. Normally, value includes some component of price, but in higher education, a larger component of "value" comes from institutional reputation. In fact, if price alone were the primary, or even a significant value driver, the community colleges of this country would be packed, and the four-year institutions would be hunting for students, even more than they do already.

When one goes out to buy a microphone to record podcasts, there are many outstanding choices. A prudent, entry-level, home-based podcaster would want a high-quality microphone that meets broadcast standards, works with most home-based systems, is easy to use and set up, and doesn't cost too much. Still, the choices for those criteria are innumerable. In that broad set of choices, other obvious considerations may come into play.

Valuing one's own time, one might elect for an online purchase so as to avoid lost time and productivity. Again, price, value, reliability, and the timeliness of delivery all must make sense. Not surprisingly, the choices are again, many. Having settled on the right product, at the right price, from a trusted brand and delivery method, all that is left is to buy the product and get it to your home. In the end of the product search, you don't really care who meets your needs of the 18 online companies who carry the exact product you want. You just want the product you desire, at the price and convenience that works so you have the tool you need for your purposes in the podcasting market.

People don't treat buying their English degree the same way. Frankly, that's reasonable, to an extent. The degree in English one might get from Rutgers versus the University of Delaware may not be the same. Each may include different program offerings, discrete courses, and particular professors who might change how one values each degree. The universities are not necessarily dramatically different in reputation, at least not to the English-degree-consuming world, which is employers looking to hire people with English degrees. However, for a person looking to obtain that degree, the emphasis on creative writing at one institution versus another might be dispositive in the choice.

All those choices and factors are reasonable—to some extent. However, as we will examine in greater detail, we must ask, is it reasonable for a child of a blue-collar New Jersey family to borrow \$120,000 to go to the University of Delaware to get an English degree if he or she could borrow \$40,000 to get an English degree from Rutgers, the state university of New Jersey? At that price differential, course offerings and the difference between creative writing classes might not be a final deciding factor.

While you ponder the wisdom of that choice, ask yourself this: What if the degree in English cost you \$252,100,[1] but it came from Harvard? Is that worth it? Having "Harvard" on your résumé is certainly worth something more than Rutgers, Delaware, or Idaho State. No one can dispute that. We will look at a checklist to drive you to value at the end of this book.

Just to complicate the issue more, imagine you are that same great New Jersey student, coming from a blue-collar family where the parents quite literally can't help you financially. All they can do is send you a few hundred bucks each semester as the budget allows. You have performed fabulously in high school, and while you are not a Harvard candidate, you certainly qualify to be admitted into either Rutgers or Delaware.

In addition, your academic record qualifies you for a special state program that will instead pay your tuition at a community college, and then pay your tuition at Rutgers if you keep a B average when you transfer to that state school. The factors driving your choice just became quite different as a much lower price now makes for a much more obvious value decision, in theory.

Under this very real-life scenario, you are looking at paying nearly zero in tuition costs, and very little in room and board if you choose the community-college-to-Rutgers choice. Indeed, you may pay only $5K to $10K to get that English degree, versus the same $120K from Delaware. Did the value decision get easier for you? Should it? You bet it should.

It is not useful to "out" the individual, but the example above is real and the product of decision making by an actual student and family. When the time came to make the choice, the student decided to go to Delaware, citing the "need" to have a "full college experience" and the desire to attend a school full time with a friend. That decision making is the product of cultural liberalism, rather than value considerations.

This family had the benefit of insight from within the educational community. Not surprisingly, the family was warned of and alerted to the costs, risks, and relative value proposition. Both blue-collar parents had the luxury of counseling on these issues from an insider. Still, they ultimately decided to support the decision of the minor to saddle debt upon the student's future. This person has long ago graduated, and after a long period of sporadic employment unrelated to the degree, or college, the individual started an entry-level job, the return of which is yet to be determined.

The debt this student has is significant. It combines guaranteed student loans and other loans cosigned, inexplicably, by the parents. One could have purchased a two-bedroom home in a nice New Jersey town in 1994 for less than this student paid for an English degree in Delaware as a resident of New Jersey. This example is a proof of the assertion that in part, the problem in higher education is sometimes us. Peer and societal pressure, sometimes tacked to parent guilt and inexperience about the issues, leave families to make catastrophically poor decisions that are based in no way on the value proposition or longer-term risks.

Putting aside the obvious, which is that the parents were neither well-versed enough, nor strong enough to make a better decision for the minor than they did, the one other not-so-obvious issue or question is this: Why does our federal government permit such debt and risk-taking with subsidized loans rather than requiring a lower-cost decision?

WHAT IS GOVERNMENT'S ROLE IN SAFEGUARDING AGAINST QUESTIONABLE LOANS?

The answer to the question, why does government allow this type of imprudent lending and debt, is simple: It is in part "cultural liberalism," which is a driving force and subset of "structural liberalism." Does the federal government want to make "value" decisions about the institution or program of study a student may take, even if the money comes from the feds? Should it do so, and if so how would it do so? Do we have a blanket right, unaccountable to anyone, other than some future debt, to study anything we want, anywhere we want, accruing the maximum allowable debt subsidized by others?

Also, in this equation, let's not forget the role of states and institutions. Delaware and its university are the revenue winners. They ring up an out-of-state student, paying a premium tuition, to help subsidize in-state tuition students. In so doing, they also use that premium to help it pay for those permanent employees ... as part of the tenure tax. Does Delaware have any obligation to counsel that student? Should it? Would Delaware raise tuition as high, or would it find cost-cutting measures if it was not the beneficiary of cheap, federally subsidized loans issued to ill-informed students? This is not to pick on the great state of Delaware. This is merely an example. This is happening in every state.

This discussion fairly brings us back to the issue of reputation. Just as some would much rather go to a higher-brand institution than an institution not quite as well known, many students and their parents are not keen on the idea of embracing community college as an interim step for their respective students. This is part stigma, part social cowardice, and mostly ignorance and ego.

Some people think community college implies a reputational black mark on the student, or worse, the parents. "Tommy is going to UVA." "Really?" "Janie is going to Tech. Did you hear that Samantha is going to Brown?" "Oh, and Brock, he's going to be at Northern Virginia Community College." What is the cost of snobbery in this equation? The truth be told, Brock might be better off getting his start at NOVA than picking an institution of much higher cost, less value, and finding out at a premium price his major was a mistake, or that he was not yet ready for the rigor or responsibility of that institution.

The book stakes out a position that "structural liberalism"—those elements that reject market principles, eschew value judgments, and disconnect consumers from risk and costs, while subsidizing universities that won't seek efficiency—is the main culprit for the spiraling cost of higher education. Each subsequent chapter in part 1 will explore this thesis.

The book will test the structural liberalism thesis as it compares market efficiency and higher education inefficiency. The examples, analogies, and anecdotes used will help demonstrate how and why educational costs are escalating at an unmatched rate, and why structural liberalism and the higher education culture of entitlement drives students needlessly to take on too much debt, or ill-advised debt for suspect degrees.

Against that backdrop, we simply cannot ignore this example. The goods and services on the American Enterprise Institute graph on the front page show that products and services subject to competition, innovation, deregulation, and market forces are all going down in price relative to regulated industries. Those prices above the line are not subject to all the components of free-market competition and pricing. They involve subsidies, redistribution, captive audiences, compelled costs, and regulation. Not surprisingly these items are spiraling out of control relative to their own value two decades ago.

Yet other industries, not heavily regulated, not subsidized, and not subject to government intervention, are providing consumers with products, services,

Figure 1.1.   Ebay advertisment. Still there:
https://www.ebay.com/itm/1996-RCA-CRT-28-PIP-COLORTRAK-PLUS-TELEVISION-Model-F27672ET-NO-REMOTE/282319886949?hash=item41bb939a65:g:Mv4AAOSw
XAJYVyGf

Figure 1.2.   Walmart advertisement.
https://www.walmart.com/ip/RCA-60-Class-FHD-1080P-LED-TV-RLED6090/54935567

and innovation that deliver better, lower-priced goods and services than they did two decades ago. If the people in higher education are so brilliant, why can't they do that? One easy answer might be that higher education's primary purpose and mission is not its consumers. In addition, the higher education industry simply is not subject to forces of efficiency for survival and is not designed to drive value and innovation to its consumers. Why the heck not?

GET THE PICTURE

In January of 1996, a rabid football fan went to a local electronics store in New Jersey and bought the best TV his money could afford. The Cowboys were playing the 49ers in the NFL playoffs and this consumer was going to watch it on an RCA 27-inch TV, in all her glory. Our consumer agreed to the steep price of $662, and wisely financed the set interest free for a year.

SHE. WAS. A. BEAUTY.

Indeed, up until two months ago she was still in use in for the consumer.[2] Here's an actual photo of that then top-of-the-line TV product (figure 1.1). Here is an RCA 60-inch, 1080P, high-definition, flat-screen TV for only $419 on sale at Walmart in April of 2017 (figure 1.2).

Which of these TVs would you like to watch?

Twenty-one years later, consumers can get a much bigger screen, much smaller TV, with much greater quality and features, for nearly $240 cheaper than in 1996. Both television sets come from the exact same manufacturer. The TV industry is neither heavily regulated nor is it subject to subsidies or redistribution. It competes on price and innovation. Makers and sellers survive by lowering costs while increasing value.

In higher education, we purportedly have the smartest people on earth in the system, and yet they have created degrees with little market value, and they are increasingly offering dubious degrees to us at much greater prices than twenty years ago. The reasons are many, but they are all related to structural liberalism. Unlike the newer TVs, it's all pretty much black and white.

Let's explore more.

Chapter 2

Does Structural Liberalism in Higher Education Serve Faculty or Students First?

The central focus of most critiques of liberalism in higher education focus on the idea and concept that politically liberal professors are "brainwashing" students with ideas antithetical to liberty, free markets, and accountability. They are. The book examines that interplay and relationship to structural liberalism in later chapters.

If the spread of a one-side ideology were the only problem in higher education, reform itself might be easier. Liberalism isn't merely the screed of social justice warriors questioning the economic underpinnings of America, it is the structure these liberals have created in the industry that has promoted higher costs, less accountability, little efficiency, and a system that graduates students with high debt and dubious skills. It is also a self-serving structure.

Ironically, liberal institutions dump students into a job market that few professors understand. Let's examine first how the economics of university politics and policy create, reward, and grow structural liberalism in a system for the primary benefit of faculty and administrators, rather than students.

If you ever want to understand what is wrong with the incentives in higher education, see if your local university will let you sit in on a faculty meeting. Professors dominate faculty meetings with discussions mostly about faculty wants, faculty needs, faculty rights, faculty pay, faculty benefits, and the need to hire more like-minded faculty.

Students rate low on the list of priorities, and to the extent faculties are talking about students, they are often talking about teaching loads, office hours, and the lack of quality students. Faculties need to either be subjected to a dictator or market forces. Market forces seem like a better solution more adaptable to the American condition.

These descriptions about faculty meetings are certainly generalizations. Make no mistake, our universities have some great professors with a strong desire to engage and teach students, and to bring their expertise to the next generation. These professors are in the minority, and even among the best of the best, the central focus of most professors in higher education is their research, their book, their project, their consulting, and their time—all of which is eaten into by the drudgery of "teaching." Mind you, as your student accrues massive debt, he or she is the drudgery in this faculty equation.

How is it that higher education has come to serve the faculty rather than the educational consumer? Let's first ask … what the heck is the Educational Consumer?

THE EDUCATIONAL CONSUMER

In 1997, an enterprising 30-year-old law student seized control of a moribund publication in his then second-tier law school.[1] It was the law school newspaper called *The Docket*.[2] He took control because, well, nobody else wanted it really. The paper had once been vibrant, but it had published only a handful of issues over the previous two years. A once proud publication, with a rebel's soul and a history of printing some terrific, biting cartoons and editorials, the paper had become fallow. That's the nature of student involvement, it ebbs and flows in any organization.

The very first thing the leadership did was to change the masthead to read "The Official Paper of the George Mason Legal Consumer." Mind you, Mason Law (Now the Scalia Law School at George Mason) was a free-market law and economics school where the faculty is libertarian to conservative, and the students were more centrist than most institutions.

Fast forward nearly 18 years from that media coup over *The Docket* newspaper. The once editor was sitting in a senior staff meeting at that same law school, now serving as an assistant dean. The dean of the law school, a brilliant, eccentric, and quite amiable man, said something that really caught the room's attention. In a short discussion about the newspaper, which had again fallen on hard times, he blurted out, "Why do they call themselves legal consumers? That's the stupidest thing I have ever heard."

The assistant dean busted out laughing, asking, why is that stupid? The dean declared, "They are students, not consumers." He went on to explain briefly that entrance into the institution was not a simple transaction open to anyone and that the term "legal consumer" denoted some market power or authority over the institution that students don't really have. Wow, the young assistant thought, he had made that tagline up 18 years earlier to stick it to the man, and look, the man is still stuck.

That dean, of course, is not completely incorrect. He is just mostly incorrect. That is, unlike walking on a car lot and agreeing to a mutual price, higher education is a complex relationship that involves a very high-priced purchase extended over time. With that purchase by the consumer comes a series of rights and responsibilities by both the student and the institution.

Firstly, the student must be of sufficient academic standing to merit even being permitted to make the investment. Nonetheless, while the consumer may be vetted by the seller, the ultimate purchase is a degree that a university confers upon the student. Yes, the student must meet a host of criteria before the degree is issued, but chief among them, after admittance, is paying the freight. Ironically, just like a car purchaser, most students don't pay cash for the degree. They finance it.

Wait, based on this description, buying that degree is nearly entirely the same as buying a car. Contrary to the belief of some educationalists, the juris doctor degree (JD) is a market commodity. Schools are in the commodity and services business. So disconnected are some inside the bubble, they have lost sight of that reality. The customer is the student, and the commodity for which they pay dearly is the degree.

In one of the most market-oriented schools in America, the idea that the educational consumer has rights and standing to demand a decent product seemed controversial. Imagine how it must be viewed elsewhere? We don't need to imagine, really, we need only examine who an institution primarily serves, and on whom the tax for that service must be levied.

In nearly every educational institution, faculty is a priority over students. That is perhaps the largest flaw in a deeply flawed higher education system. Every single decision made by institutions comes with costs. When an institution of higher learning creates programs, hires faculty, tenures faculty, invests in infrastructure, or even apportions resources, it creates costs. Someone must bear those costs.

In the educational industry costs are borne by students who pay for the right to attend the institution. Of course, others contribute to the pot of money that runs an institution. You have federal research grants, donations, state subsidies, and subsidized student loans. It is a complex system, and it is getting increasingly complex each day.

Universities have become revenue predators, seeking cash to offset rising expenses by any means possible. They rent space to outside groups, they offer non-degree and certificate programs. They create "academic" centers funded by third-party interest groups. They lobby state legislators, federal regulators, and even accrediting bodies. Their "advancement" operations, which used to be called "development," and before that "fundraising," are sophisticated machines that target alumni donations, corporate giving, and major gifts. As we expose later, so desperate for cash are many of these operations that they trade long-term debt obligations for short-term cash.

In some institutions, the development teams have a price for everything in the university, just in case of a "naming" opportunity. None of these realities make universities suspect or even shady. If programs have value, and if consumers are willing to purchase those programs, or the altruistic are willing to give, that is great. However, the drive for cash has never been stronger, endowments have never been bigger, yet tuition continues to skyrocket at every institution. Why?

Structural liberalism drives the cost of higher education. Over the next set of chapters, we will examine how "liberal" choices in programing, administration, and university governance drive costs. We will look at what I call the tenure tax. Arguably, the chapters ahead expose the practical and unkind reality that higher education has a social justice warrior tax. It has a lack of productivity tax. It has a geriatric tax. It certainly has a cronyism tax. And they have a liberal philosophy tax.

Each of these taxes comes from a central principle that causes the educational bureaucracy to do what any inefficient bureaucracy does: It puts the needs of the bureaucracy first, the wants of the bureaucracy second, and the service of the customer last. It is less of an evil plan than the unfortunate reality of a liberal design.

Incentives matter. Those who run universities have little incentive to change the beneficiaries—because it is them.

Chapter 3

Do You Want a K-Car or a Porsche?

The 1982 Porsche 911—there was no substitute. Its MSRP? ($30,000).

When you enroll at a university as a freshman, such as the University of Maryland or George Mason University in Virginia, you probably pay tuition. Some students earn scholarships for a whole host of reasons, legitimate and otherwise. However, even if you get financial aid, a grant, or a scholarship, that university has a fixed tuition. Your student account gets billed that tuition, among other charges and fees. Schools then apply your bill against any aid or scholarship, and the balance left is to be borne by the educational consumer.

Let's say the incoming full-time tuition for the fall semester is $5,862,[1] or $11,724 for the year, minus room, board, books, and other fees. You pay that same tuition if your major is dance, engineering, physics, cybersecurity, applied global conservation, applied mathematics, women and gender studies, nursing, finance, or social justice and human rights.[2]

One education, one price, one value. That's how they do it, and in fact that is how nearly every institution does it. Without political commentary, do we think the degree in women and gender studies will return the same economic market value as degrees in finance, nursing, or engineering?

The 1982 Dodge Aries K.—proving the 1980s were great for music, not for cars. Its MSRP? ($6,300).

Now, the fair critique of this rhetorical question is that not everyone is going into finance or nursing, and people ought not to be forced to study something they don't like. Moreover, some will tell you, and argue quite forcefully, that subjects like women and gender studies play a pivotal role in transforming society, and that all education has an intrinsic and personal value. It may well be, as the argument goes, that those who study women and gender studies will live a more rewarding and fulfilling life. Perhaps.

Figure 3.1. The 1982 Dodge Aries K.—proving the 1980s were great for music, not for cars. Its MSRP? ($6,300).
From blog post: https://blog.dodge.com/heritage/1982-dodge-aries/

This analysis doesn't posit the idea that any one form of education is bad, *per se*. Majors have an individual value to each person in the major. That is undoubtedly true. However, these educations have costs, and they have market values. The cost is fixed and identical, but the market values are not.

Plainly stated, however one values his or her humanities degree—in whatever juicy or trendy topic—the degree has a value to employers. These degrees are simply less valuable in the marketplace, collectively, than other degrees. In fact, easily available data show that traditionally tough majors immediately have a better starting salary. Not surprisingly, computer science, electrical engineering, and mechanical engineering continue to be among the leaders.[3]

As dubious majors expand, their cost is just as expensive to obtain from the same institution where other graduates obtain better market skills. However, not only does the dubious major get saddled with debt, but all tuition payers are saddled with the cost of these dubious majors in their respective bills.

Figure 3.2.   The 1982 Porsche 911—there was no substitute. Its MSRP? ($30,000).
Car sale posting: http://www.cardomain.com/ride/3364290/1982-porsche-911/

Let's look at these great cars pictured at the beginning of this chapter. The 1982 Dodge Aries K (figure 3.1) may be the ugliest car any design engineer ever conjured up from a nightmare. However, if one wanted cheap transportation, that car did the trick. Likewise, the Porsche 911 (figure 3.2), would also provide that transportation.

Somewhere in this fair land lives at least one human being who looks at the Aries K and is starry-eyed. It is the car of his or her dreams. For that person, to have, to hold, to buff, or to drive that car is the culmination of a dream, and such an experience exceeds the value of any other car-driving experience. That person is out there, and he or she probably lives next door to the person who thinks Brussels sprouts are better than ice cream.

However, for the overwhelming majority of consumers, they would prefer to own the Porsche. In fact, not only would that be an accurate assessment of popular sentiment unnecessary to subject to empirical study, but the market too values the Porsche considerably more. Indeed, that's your empirical proof.

The Porsche is built better, has more features, provides more options, a better ride, more speed, and more style. More people want it, and therefore it costs more. Heck, it costs a lot more. That is because no matter how one feels about his or her personal favorite vehicle, all cars have a market value. Like a solid degree, decades later these cars still have market values, and those market values reflect the proven quality over time. The classic Aries K from 1982 now has, if in good condition, a classic car, retail average value of $1,200.[4] The 1982 Porsche has an average retail value of $35,000.[5] A great product, be it a car or a valuable education, holds its value over time.

Education, too, has a market value. So why are universities charging the same tuition for majors of entirely different values? The answer is cultural liberalism, a key component of structural liberalism. We might also ask, why does the government lend taxpayer-subsidized student loans at the same rate for the same risk to these less valued majors?

As discussed earlier, these prices for degrees change by and between different universities. An English degree from Harvard costs more than an English degree from George Mason. In that instance, you are paying for the word "Harvard" on your degree. You are paying handsomely too. We can and should discuss if that investment is wise. However, few would ever dispute that the market value of a Harvard English degree, whatever it might be, is certainly higher than the market value of a George Mason English degree. That's no knock on the fine educational professionals at Mason. The world values the Porsche over the K-Car, and we understand that reality with little need for an explanation.

However, the question posed here is simple: Does George Mason, Temple, the University of Maryland, Mary Washington, Radford—pick a school, nearly any school—think that the value of each and every one of its majors is the same? I hope not. The only people on earth who think the market value of an engineering degree from Mason is the same as the market value of a degree in women and gender studies are people disconnected from reality. The study of women may be endless, and more complicated than engineering, but the degree one obtains in it simply is without the same market strength to employers.

Why don't universities charge different tuitions for different majors?

The answer—as you might have guessed—is in major part due to structural liberalism.

Chapter 4

What Is the Tenure Tax?

More than a year ago, in writing this book, the phrase "tenure tax" first emerged. The book mentions it already, and it is time we discuss what it is, and what is meant by it. To understand why and how tenure is a tax, and indeed an unnecessary tax on educational consumers, we need to examine what tenure is, and how one becomes tenured.

Tenure is a process of job protection. The system of granting tenure works generally the same at every public and private institution. On the margins, there may be slight differences, but the result of the process is primarily the same. Universities build their teaching, scholarship, and research around finding top talent, evaluating scholars, and through an academic procedure, offering something called "tenure" to those they deem the best.

Nearly everything about tenure in higher education is a disaster for the educational consumer. It's a bad bet for the institutions as well. The very small benefits of granting tenure are far outweighed by the burdens and costs of granting it. Without tenure reform—and thus a tenure tax cut—Americans can never reduce the cost of higher education. No other higher education reform is as critical to reform or revolution in the industry as overhauling tenure.

A tenured professor is nearly impossible to fire. Certainly, when one writes this, an academic will pop up and cite the case of one person, or maybe remind others that each university has a process called post-tenure review. In short, technically speaking, tenured faculty can lose their respective jobs, but it is exceedingly rare. Indeed, more people are likely abducted by UFOs each year than the number of tenured professors fired for noncriminal activity.

While the grant of tenure comes from the university, it is only after a vote and approval process by the faculty. Indeed, the faculty run the entire process from recruitment, to interviewing, and selecting prospective new faculty

Rich Kelsey @RichKelsey · 26 Dec 2016
U know just 2 of the reasons why college tuition costs far outpace cpi ... dubious majors & permanent professors. #tenuretax

Jonathan H. Adler ● @jadler1969
Crazy or evil?
University Professor: I Want 'White Genocide' For Christmas
dailycaller.com/2016/12/25/uni... via @dailycaller

Figure 4.1.
Link to tweet: https://twitter.com/RichKelsey/status/813416725672849410.

members. Once blessed into a faculty, professional academics don't often work to unseat their brethren, even those with whom they have no agreement. It's a union or brotherhood.

To be clear, tenure is supposed to be reserved for the top talent, with the most elite skills in their given field. In some institutions, people are tenured for their teaching, some for their grant-funded research, and some for their scholarship. Indeed, in most cases, it is a combination of two or more of those factors.

In a law school, for example, one may lateral in as a "tenured" professor, or one may be hired in the "tenure line." The tenure line means a professor is new and is in line to be tenured provided the hired candidate meets the expectations of the faculty over a given time. Law schools will hire a new professor with brilliant academic credentials and often a high-end judicial clerkship. Many new tenure-line faculty members in law schools have clerked at federal courts of appeals or even the Supreme Court. They also have produced well-regarded academic research. That research tends to complement the work of existing faculty members.

Prospective professors appear at job talks, and they present either finished or working papers to other professors. This system permits the sharing of intellectual pursuits, and it allows a faculty to judge the quality of the scholarship and the ability of the professor to defend it.

Ultimately, it is nearly impossible to be granted tenure without first getting the approval of a hiring committee of the faculty of an institution and a vote from the full faculty. Of course, once that's done, the university administration must approve the candidate and hire him or her.

If it is a lateral hire of a candidate previously tenured by another institution, he or she comes in "tenured." If the hire is a new, "tenure-line" professor, then tenure is granted later. It is true that sometimes a tenure-line hire does not achieve or earn tenure. However, once tenured, professors are only terminated under the most extraordinary circumstances, such as criminality, or alien abduction.

WHAT ARE THE REASONS FOR TENURE?

The best explanation for tenure is that it permits scholars and teachers of such high and proven talent to focus and concentrate on their research and academic pursuits without falling to the whims of academic or political retaliation. A professor does not have to worry about the pettiness or smallness of one administrator who might want to fire him or her simply because of a spat or a disagreement over scholarship or politics. In America, it is sometimes said, only tenured law professors, retirees, and billionaires have free speech.

Tenure is lifetime. Most institutions do not have restraints on tenure, though some have moved to a system of mandatory retirement based upon age. As a practical matter, no mechanism of which I am aware does more to protect employees than tenure granted professors by universities. Tenured professors are highly compensated, they work very leisurely schedules, and while they may have required duties, they essentially can't be compelled to do much.

For example, professors often have a credit-hour requirement for the academic year. The overwhelming majority teach in the field in which they study and research, while junior professors often take the more generic and less sought-after classes in a university.

Critics of tenure will often point to egregious examples of political activism and outrageous statements. The problem with tenure is not so much that it produces some screwballs with a license to use their academic freedom as a platform for tomfoolery, it is that the system that best protects academic freedom is an economic disaster for those who must fund it. That is the educational consumer.

LIFETIME TENURE IS FUNDED BY YOUR TUITION

Many parents are just now paying tuition bills. One parent just paid his first tuition bill for his oldest daughter who went off to college in the fall of 2017. It was about $4,400. (That's just tuition, not including housing, meals, fees, etc. All-in, semester one was about $10,500.) She goes to a state school, which means that the state subsidizes the school. That really means that some portion of the institution's annual overhead costs are prepaid by the taxpayers of the state. It is the same in every state.

Why do states "subsidize" these tuitions? This is a system every state uses, and the states do so for good reasons. The goal is to make tuition affordable for your residents, to encourage them to stay, and thus invest in a workforce that can graduate, contribute, and help build economic prosperity in the state.

These state subsidies reduce the balance of the operational costs of the university and what is left to pay, either for debt or operations, sets the price of your tuition. Nonprofit schools don't make a "profit," and hence each year the various forms of revenue, most being tuition, go to operational expenses.

The single biggest driver of cost in any university is its professors, and in particular, its tenure line. They are a permanent cost. At Mason Law, the majority of the budget went to paying its employees, with the overwhelming majority going to our tenured professors. Now, that doesn't mean that Mason is grossly overpaying professors. Indeed, in many institutions, particularly the cash-starved universities, professors' pay is not comparable to other similarly ranked schools.

Throw in the cost of living, and accepting the offer of becoming a law professor, for example, at Mason Law is a great job. It is not the highest and best use of the skills of every professor. Indeed, from professors to most associate and assistant deans in law schools, many of those talented staff take pay cuts to work in these jobs. Still, highly compensated people will take the lower pay for the easier hours, unmatched benefits, innumerable holidays, and passion for the work, of course. Professors and even lowly assistant deans can often make more money in a market with higher risks and greater demands. More importantly, for professors in the tenure line, the job protectionism can never be matched in the private sector.

Pay, of course, is only one factor in any compensation. How good are the fringe benefits for the tenured class? Some universities budget 35 percent of a base salary as additional compensation and overhead. A university, of course, always reminds its employees each year that while they are being paid X, they have a total compensation of Y. A quick look at law school salary might be useful.

A junior law professor might be hired at $110,000 for a 9-month contract (that's roughly equivalent to $146,000 per full year). However, that $110,000 really cost the university $148,500 with benefits. Indeed, as healthcare costs rise, so does the cost of the benefits. If you look back at the graph on the cover of this book, you will note that healthcare, another highly regulated, quasi-socialist set of products and services, ranks high on busting the CPI. The rising cost of healthcare for a permanent class of growing employees who don't have to retire only acts to exponentially increase the costs of higher education.

WHAT MAKES TENURE A TAX?

You may call tenure a "cost," but it is more accurate to consider tenure a tax. Universities must have professors. As such, they must be paid. To that extent, professors' salaries are a cost. Good universities pay good money to great professors. That cost is passed on to the educational consumer in his or her bill. The tax is the cost of the tenure and the inefficiency it brings. Tenure is a penalty on the tuition payer. It's both the real cost of the operational overhead for the skills necessary to deliver the services, plus a surcharge or tax for the lifetime employment, the lost opportunity costs, and the inefficiency of the system. It is, in a sense, the tax one must pay that would not exist if hiring professors were a market-based activity.

Unlike a tax that one might pay for common services, the tenure tax is really a tax that all students must pay for a system that does not permit universities to fire, downsize, right-size, or economize their faculties. Moreover, because the employee may stay and continue working well past his or her most productive years, it is a steep and increasing tax as operational productivity drops.

Indeed, the tenure tax gets even more steep when one considers that productivity drops as we age, and that the hidden cost of benefits continues to rise.[1] Tenure is the ultimate market manipulator. Businesses that cannot change their employees, reward production, punish inefficiency, and change to meet market demand are certain to face skyrocketing costs. Indeed, the tenure is worse than one might think.

When a law school, for example, realizes that it has an entire faculty that focuses on law and economics, a worthwhile and thoughtful set of analytical tools, but that it needs faculty to teach privacy law, cyberlaw, or some other emerging area that might attract students and help graduates obtain jobs, it must hire more faculty. The school can't look at the faculty and say, all right, this person is researching in an area of no interest and produces little or no scholarship, we will replace him. No, the institution must keep the inefficiency and then add to it with the new areas of expertise. That is a tax on tuition payers.

No business on earth would survive in such a system, yet universities keep chugging along. They do so by raising prices, getting subsidies, encouraging the government to grant low-interest loans to consumers, and by hunting for revenue through creating and foisting on students degrees, programs, and majors of little market value.

Figure 4.2.
http://wikiboombox.com/tiki-index.php?page=Sony+CFS-67.

Remember those car comparisons? What would each car cost if the manufacturers had to keep paying all the employees for as long as they wanted to work, and only for the type of work they wanted to do?

What if Sony had to keep making the Boombox (figure 4.2) or the Walkman (figure 4.3)?

This 1980s vintage gem was the true innovation in music delivery in her time. Later, the world fell in love with music on the move.

Now imagine that every employee, from designer, to engineer, to the production team for Sony had to keep building these products and only these products. To move from the Boombox to the Walkman, Sony had to hire different teams. Then, no matter what Sony did, it had to hire new people for the new products and services *while* it kept the old team and still paid them. Would that model work?

Now you understand the tenure tax in its simplest terms.

EXAMPLES OF THE TENURE TAX

It is not the purpose of this analysis to pick on law schools, let alone a law school that has been traditionally quite efficient when compared to many other schools. However, the faculty at Mason Law is also a tenured faculty.

Figure 4.3.
https://www.amazon.com/Sony-WM-FS221-Sports-Walkman-Cassette/dp/
B000067FC5.

Of course it is. One former associate dean from that institution used to call tenured faculty "the union." That union can't be busted.

Mason Law is teeming with strong academics and legal expertise. The faculty is considered elite, and based upon the usage and downloads of their scholarship, the faculty ranks quite high relative to many other faculties. One ranking has Mason Law routinely in the top 25, or even in the teens based on what professors call "scholarly impact."

What is "scholarly impact"? Professors publish books and scholarly articles. Those articles are made available for download, and the downloads are tracked. Much like websites track unique page views to assign a value to the content, the academic industry tracks downloads for the same purpose.

Anyone downloading a scholarly article is almost certainly reading it and putting it to use in school, practice, or a legal opinion. Unlike political blogging, the readers of scholarly work, while a much smaller and discrete group, are reading past the titles and not looking for clickbait.

Still, while Mason Law has built a scholarship culture, it has one of the lowest teaching load requirements in the industry. Not surprisingly, among its many outstanding professors, some are more prolific writers than others. Some produce little new scholarship and are functionally much less productive than others.

It is also not surprising that as with any given group in a system that does not reward efficiency and production or punish inefficiency, some professors are certainly less productive than one might want if one were running an institution in an industry with a significant problem attracting consumers.

Before departing Mason Law, an assistant dean performed an analysis of the institution to see how it might save money on faculty "if" the university could work out a deal for early retirement, somehow convincing a certain set of professors to take the deal. Frankly, what incentive would a professor have to forgo the deal he or she already had? Right now, a professor can keep working until 90, or death, and keep getting paid.

Nonetheless, the analysis was performed because the institution, like most law schools, was bleeding cash—hemorrhaging, really—and student applications and enrollment were down. The analysis was not commissioned by the dean, but instead was an initiative of his management and planning dean that stemmed from attending university-wide meetings on administrative matters. At one such meeting, the university pried open the door to an early retirement package. That university initiative was the catalyst for examining how "efficiency," based on performance, cost, and subject matter need, might benefit Mason Law if it wanted to try to find a way to attack the sunk tenure tax costs.

How bad were the losses at Mason Law at that time? It was burning losses of nearly $2 million a year, with only $6 million or so in reserves. A responsible administration not only had to find more revenue and attract more students, it also needed to consider cost-cutting options. Most universities, because of the reality of tenure, are forced only to hunt revenue, rather than attack their biggest cost—tenured faculty. The quick analysis was designed to seize a unique opening to try to do both.

An assistant dean, with a business background, thought proactively of looking at "what-if" scenarios that might be an option if they could be wrapped into the early retirement package. As any executive would, he considered how to cut unnecessary cost, even if it took upfront investment to shave lifetime cost. The head of the unit, the big dean, hit delete on that idea. However, the reality was a simple math equation.

Since the dean nixed the idea, this book revives it here and gives the readers some idea of how the missing efficiency in structural liberalism prevents attacking the actual costs and the lost opportunity costs they can also create. That former academic unit dean is now retired back into the faculty, and the analysis is updated to include him.

The former dean at Mason Law is well regarded in the industry, and by any objective measure he was a very fine dean. He was a brilliant academic prior to rising to the level of full dean. Internally, he was mostly responsible for the school's rise in the *US News* rankings because of his analysis of the rankings methodology and his efforts to move Mason's strengths to the places where it could best improve its rank.

The dean served for nearly a decade, and his salary as dean of the law school was over $320,000. Given his responsibilities, the size of the budget, and the importance of the role, the salary for his position at the institution, in that market, was not controversial.

When the dean decided to step back from the role of dean of the law school and return to function solely as a professor, many in that administration and faculty were disappointed. Replacing a low-ego dean with proven experience, steady leadership, and confidence in his professional staff was certainly a high-risk event, and one many were concerned about given the very difficult financial times on which most law schools, particularly Mason, had fallen.

At a designated time, and after a search and replacement, the dean left his post and returned to the faculty where he still serves, and where he will continue to serve until he decides to leave, or his maker calls him home. The dean's new salary is … the same.

The dean is not a prolific scholar anymore, and he teaches a lighter load. His teaching is fine, but not exceptional by any rank or standard. He does not raise money. His total compensation is over $400,000 and will be for years to come. With that money, Mason could hire two midlevel professors with fire in their bellies and expertise and scholarship in emerging areas of the law. Instead, Mason, and its students, are left paying the tenure tax. The former dean's total compensation is nearly a $1,000-per-year tax on every JD candidate student.

The analysis performed on Mason's faculty looked at a way to induce professors like the dean to leave, and thus address these costs and productivity issues. It considered downsizing six professors, not including the now ex-dean. Had the analysis included the dean, Mason Law could be saving over 1.5 million dollars a year. That alone would have brought it closer to being financially sound at the time when applications continued to fall, and the necessary class size, and hence revenue, simply was not there to support the school's overhead.

In the 2014 and 2015 years, Mason Law had enrolled back-to-back classes of approximately 150 students. In fact, enrollments in law schools were down nearly 45 percent from their all-time high nationally. Cutting costs was one obvious method to stay competitive to help attract a dwindling pool of law applicants.

At the time of the analysis, total enrollment was down to about 475 students from nearly 650. Yet the total number of permanent, tenured faculty remained roughly the same. The student population was down roughly 37 percent, but the analysis looked to reduce the tenured faculty by only 15 to 16 percent. The result of that analysis would have saved every student in the building more than $3,000 each year if the savings were applied back to the educational consumer.

If one were to poll the average Mason Law student or any student from any similar institution, and students were asked if they would like to save $9,000 off the cost of their three-year law degree, nearly 100 percent would say yes. If the analysis were forced to tell the students the names of the people who would take early retirement in the plan to achieve those costs, probably 99.9 percent would have said, ok, great. The analysis never went anywhere past the dean.

In fact, the dean initially rejected the unsolicited idea suggesting that the university could not offer such a package even if he wanted because the retirement buy-down is a state-controlled formula not subject to enhancements. While facially correct, each of those professors could have signed a legal settlement with the university that would have had them leave, the terms of which would have included the buy-down, effectuating the same result. A legal settlement would have end-run the University and state early retirement process.

So Mason could have tried to do it—if it wanted to cut costs. If serving the educational consumer were in the primary interest of the institution, such a plan would have been well received. Keeping high-income, underperforming, tenured faculty, however, was a greater priority. Again, because structural liberalism prioritizes faculty over students and consumers.

A dean also understands he or she really works at the pleasure of the union, and he is also a union member. Did I forget to mention that "the dean" of an institution is also a tenured member of the faculty?

Incentives matter, and downsizing certainly would have had other implications for Mason Law. No one can deny that fact. For example, it would have sent a market signal of weakness for the institution, and it may well have had a chilling effect on future recruiting of faculty if recruits thought Mason would work to unload them when times were tough.

Still, universities not only can't think and act outside the box, but they don't really want to do so in many cases. Those tasked with making the decisions are not ever going to act against their own interest.[2] This again brings us back to the question: Whose interest does a faculty primarily serve? Add to that question, whose interest does a tenured faculty's dean really serve in this system of structural liberalism? In the scenario set out above, it's clear that the interests of underperforming, highly compensated professors trump the debt loads of those stuck paying the tenure tax.

OTHER REASONS TENURE IS A BAD BARGAIN FOR THE EDUCATIONAL CONSUMER

A tenured professor must be smart. That's literally and figuratively. With tenure, an institution is locked into an employee for life. However, the employee can leave whenever he or she wants to go. The schools certainly can't force them to stay, and a professor's tenure comes as an agreement, but that doesn't include a length of service. In fact, even with professors whose compensation is paid entirely through research grants, the grant will leave the university in most cases with the professor if he or she departs, so even grant money can't make a professor stay.

No competent entity should want an employee who doesn't want to stay, and this book does not argue that professors ought not to be permitted to leave. In fact, no agreement would be valid that required professors to stay. The analysis merely points out that the tenure bargain is so lopsided that the valued employee can leave with two weeks' notice or stay until he or she is 90 or beyond. With tenure, an institution has all the risk, none of the flexibility, and only the hope that it receives a reward.

Professors do jump around, and like most people, they chase money, resources, quality of life, and prestige. Sometimes, like regular folk, they leave for family reasons. However, they leave when it suits them, and they get to stay whether it suits the university or not. If the academic bargain doesn't work out for the institution, the cost of that arrangement is paid for by the students, not the university. This is the tenure tax. Just like corporations, universities don't really pay taxes. They pass the cost of any tax on to consumers.

Universities do a pay a different price for the inflexibility of tenure, which again is a tax ultimately borne by tuition payers. Institutions, stuck with permanent employee and sunk costs, simply cannot move swiftly to meet real market needs and reduce costs, which are the best ways to attract students. Here's an example.

Chapter 4

THE TENURE TAX AND LOST OPPORTUNITY COSTS

Imagine you run a first-tier law school in a great but competitive legal market. Your geographical competitors have more money, and in two of the four cases, they have much greater prestige and national rank. You are in an industry where consumers are scarce for all competitors, and you need consumers. Moreover, if you don't want your institution's rank to fall, you will need to attract a certain type of high-quality student. For you, it's not just bodies. You must have students of a certain quality or your institution, teetering on the edge of the critical consumer rankings, will fall from the top tier. If it does, that will assure that your institution will receive far fewer top-quality applicants in the next recruiting cycle.

That law school, of course, is Mason Law. Up until around 2003 or 2004, Mason Law was a true bargain. It had location, price, and an outstanding reputation. After years of the university hiking tuition and taking the "profit" from the law school to subsidize other units, the school found itself in a down legal education market, with high overhead and fewer customers. Its competitors had more resources, better reputations, and a broader array of revenue-contributing programs.

In this reality created by the down legal market, Mason Law was left with a great reputation and location, but no longer a price advantage in the market. The university increased prices nearly 10 percent every year, which is the functional equivalent of doubling tuition every 7.2 years. Mason Law knew and still knows that if it falls in the *US News* rankings, it will have only location left to market to the high-quality educational consumers it needs. That makes the selling tougher when it once had price, reputation, and location to market.

What a school like Mason Law needs is innovation. It needs to offer opportunities that are emerging in the law and take advantage of its location in doing so. That's not terribly sophisticated analysis. However, if you have permanent employees, rising costs, and falling revenue, how do you make these new innovative offerings? Tenure has now handicapped your ability to innovate without finding outside or private money. This is the operational and strategic handicapping effect that a tenure tax has on the institution itself. Tenure creates lost opportunity costs.

At Mason, it found innovation with respect to a Center for the Protection of Intellectual Property, which focuses on intellectual property as a personal property right. Mason's location near two technology corridors, the Patent and Trade Office, and lobbying firms and companies interested in such protection gave rise to a center that serves an academic function, expands the school's offerings, enhances its reputation, and brings in private money.

However, not every innovation can or should be funded by private money, and as I discuss in a later chapter, not all private money is truly costless. With efficiencies not available to universities because of tenure, smart schools do what they can. What Mason really needs, and it has needed for some time, is a core curriculum focusing on cyberlaw, regulation, cybersecurity, and privacy law. These are and will continue to be hot areas in which an increasingly tech-savvy student body is interested. In addition, these skills and expertise have real demand even in a down-market legal market.

Mason has adjunct offerings around these topics, but it cannot create and market a program that would draw in top students. Why? It has too many tenure-line professors writing articles about law and economics on esoteric subjects about which professors care but about which an employment market does not. That's a problem. Those resources cannot be recaptured through the traditional business practices of right-sizing, downsizing, or reallocating resources.

Since professorial skills are not fungible, Mason must either make and absorb more sunk costs, or forgo the opportunity. Mason can try to muddle through with adjuncts and part-timers. In fact, in my model, such term experts would be hired without tenure. However, it is tenure that is the obstacle because the resources necessary to hire the right nontenured personnel are tied up on tenured personnel.

To launch a nationally successful program that might attract more students, you need more assets and expertise working full time and exclusively on building such a program. Having permanent employees tied up with outdated skills and expertise, such that an institution cannot effectively innovate, is another consequence of the tenure tax. While student loan borrowers pay the cost of the tenure tax in debt, the university pays it in lost opportunity costs. All of that is because structural liberalism elevates the needs of faculty over the needs and interests of student consumers.

Chapter 5

Who Is Running This Place?

FRIENDS DON'T LET FRIENDS HIRE FRIENDS

Universities have many structures of governance. Most have a president, a provost, and a senior management team that includes various officers from COOs to CFOs. In most universities, the president ultimately reports to a board of trustees or visitors. In the public schools of Virginia, for example, the governor appoints a board of visitors to each public institution, and ultimately those visitors have the final power in the university. It is the president and his team, with the deans below that team, who purportedly "run" the universities' day-to-day operations. These universities may be billion-dollar a-year enterprises, like George Mason.

Who really runs the university, though?

When a former CEO and big-firm lawyer returned to become an assistant dean at his law school, his boss stopped by one day to ask him how he was adjusting to university life. The former assistant dean noted he was getting used to the pace, but that he found attending intercampus, agenda-less, liaison-style meetings to be frustrating. The former executive said he was "getting used to being in middle management." The dean laughed and said, "It's worse than you think. I am middle management, you just work for me." They all work for the union, and that union is the tenured faculty that run every university.

For some, this is a radical notion. Indeed, many essays and op-eds have been written suggesting that universities are run by an "army of deans." Most deans, however, aren't generals. They aren't majors either. They are foot-soldiers, and they work for the collective. Administrative deans can slow down progress and hold you hostage to rules, regulations, and pointless meetings, but they can be replaced, easily. An at-will dean is not a general.[1]

Here is a strange reality: Many universities have innumerable "deans" running around. We have assistant deans, associate deans, and senior associate deans. The administrative cost of higher education is another factor in escalating tuitions. Ironically, those administrative costs are, by and large, foisted on universities by parents. The book discusses this truth in the next chapter. The point here is, universities have people with many fancy titles, but they really aren't in charge of much. That may be an oversimplification, but the reality is they are not in charge of much that matters financially or strategically. Outwardly, students and the public might wrongly think that deans stand above faculty. The public may wrongly think that deans direct the schools in which they work, and the faculty ultimately works for them. That's a hoot.

Faculties don't even work for the actual dean. Each individual unit has a dean, and that dean is also a tenured faculty member. He or she is the administrative head of his or her unit. All the "under-deans," by any title, wield no power of any kind. The big dean is just one vote in a faculty. An unhappy faculty will revolt, and they will and do get deans fired from the role of dean. (Note, deans can't get fired from being a faculty member, so a "fired" dean returns to faculty, retires, or moves on to another faculty if he or she desires.)

A full dean is not without power. He can assign classes, office space, research money, and the like. He can make the life of a faculty member miserable, to an extent. The level of misery he or she can inflict is limited to the willingness of the rest of the union to see another member take his or her lumps. Mostly, taking on faculty in a significant way is a surefire recipe for a dean getting nothing done and ultimately being squeezed out.

Who runs your university? By and large, the faculty do. That's not good. Faculties are smart, but as a group, they are detached, indifferent, spoiled, pampered, underworked, and completely and totally self-interested. We are all self-interested; I suppose the better description of tenured faculty is self-serving. Now, that's not a fair description of every faculty member at every school. However, as a group that is the vast peloton. In fact, the tenure system insulates and cements these characteristics.

Tenure itself is about the faculty member individually and not the institution. The structure of tenure, as I explained, provides all the benefit and reward to the faculty member and all the risk and cost to the institution. So why wouldn't a faculty member be self-serving? They were created to be so.

Faculty that serves itself first puts everyone else second.

That means, at the end of the day in higher education, the primary function and incentive system is to feed faculty and serve their interests, rather than to serve the interests of students who are the customers. This, by the way, is classic progressive, big-government elitism at work. The superior take care of themselves, and they ration for the rest that to which the elite think those below them deserve.

If institutional suffering should be felt, it should be felt among the little people. When your tuition soars, faculty will complain about a lack of funding, failures in fundraising, administrative bloat, inequities among units, but they never, not once ever, consider the cost of the tenure tax on your bill and higher education. What they have is an entitlement, and what you must pay might be unfair for you, but it's the cost of having them.

Who hires tenured faculty members in a university? Well, tenured faculty hires faculty members. The dean might appoint an adjunct, he might appoint, with faculty approval, a term faculty[2] member, but the dean doesn't hire faculty. He might recommend faculty, and if he has the support of his faculty, the faculty might accept that recommendation. Deans, however, don't hire tenured faculty. They only control administrative hiring, and even in that area, they can be handcuffed by some state rules with certain types of wage and hourly employees. For example, it is easier for a dean to replace an administrative dean, such as an assistant dean, than it is to reassign or release classified or hourly employees in a state system.

Is that any way to run a business?

What do you get when faculty hire faculty? You get the priorities of faculty over the priorities of the university and students. You get friends, or political or philosophical friends and soulmates invited into a lifetime club. In that club, no one gets to tell them what to research or how to prioritize their work with the needs of an institution for the express purposes of serving and attracting customers.

No competent business or service provider could work, thrive, and survive in the model of hiring used by universities. The system is particularly egregious when, as with many higher education institutions, funding is subsidized by public dollars and there is an element of public trust. Why do we permit the employees of an institution to hire people that serve the wishes, interest, and political philosophy of the employees, rather than the needs of the customer or the priorities of the institution's leaders? Higher education not only does that, it is almost exclusively the manner in which it functions. That is a defining characteristic of structural liberalism.

HIRING PEOPLE YOU KNOW

Every business, at some point, hires people based on relationships. This book does not suggest that if exceptionally talented faculty members know and respect the work of a prospective faculty applicant that such an applicant should not be hired. That's silly. This author was hired back to his university because most people in the building knew him and his skills, and they understood his unique relationship to the school.

The difference in the example here is that faculties are hiring permanent, lifetime employees of a type or philosophy without regard to the role or needs of the university. When a nontenured administrator is hired, he or she at least can be fired and replaced if the role or needs change, or someone with better skills becomes available. Likewise, a nontenured employee can ultimately be fired and replaced. The point is, administrative bloat might be bad, but it is fixable, as administrators are replaceable.

Returning to an earlier example, Mason Law has an enormous number of scholars researching and writing in the broad field of law and economics. Within that field, they have numerous members writing on property rights, free markets, deregulation, and matters related to antitrust. One prominent faculty member once remarked, "I dare say we (Mason Law) have the best antitrust faculty of any law school in the world." In legal parlance, that is called sales puffery, from the great carbolic smoke machine case.[3]

Putting aside the validity of the statement, which is hard to dispute, the issue with George Mason's faculty is that it keeps building that expertise for its own purposes, yet it produces only a handful of graduates in that field. Moreover, no major firm or firms are tripping over themselves to get to the students produced from this purported reservoir of expertise. Antitrust lawyers are rare, and the field itself is in very small demand relative to the size of the legal market. That is not to say that antitrust lawyers with proven skills are not in high demand, but law students from a lower-first law school who study antitrust from a faculty of law and econ scholars are not in high demand. Antitrust lawyers are smart, they are elite, and they are a tiny fraction of a legal market often gleaned from the most elite institutions and clerkships.

There is not one scintilla of evidence to suggest legal employers are flocking to Mason for this expertise. In addition, there is no meaningful evidence to suggest prospective, high-caliber applicants, in any worthwhile number, are applying to Mason Law because of this faculty expertise. If Mason Law were yielding additional student recruits of the necessary academic pedigree from this investment made on more antitrust professors, some measure of the costs might be justified. It is not.

George Mason needs to offer courses and concentrations in areas of the law where jobs and opportunities are hot, growing, and plentiful. Yet when the hiring committee gets together, they are looking for law and econ scholars focused on the same philosophy and subject areas that complement the work of the existing faculty. Can we blame the faculty for this? Maybe we should, but we really can't. The tenure system that higher education designed encourages this self-interest, and any sensible tenured faculty member who is a part of such a system would naturally gravitate toward like-minded people whose research and work extends their own.

How some law student gets a job after he or she graduates once again would not be the top priority of faculty decisions taken by faculty. Faculty has a job, and they want their job to be better.

That is why you don't put the employees in charge of hiring, and that is why you don't create employees one cannot fire or reassign when an institution needs to meet the ever-changing demands and market for its customers.

THE POLITICS OF THE TENURE CLASS

This book has a provocative title; if it were an online op-ed, it might even be called clickbait. That's because many people read and view phrases from their own phenomenology. We're probably all guilty of that. When one reads "Liberalism" with "Higher Education" one might think the central focus of the book is about the proliferation of what we call modern, political "liberalism," or for this book's purpose, what I call "cultural liberalism," which is a political ideology common among colleges and professors. Too many articles and far too many books have been written on that subject. Still, "cultural liberalism" is a natural part and offshoot of "structural liberalism."

"CULTURAL LIBERALISM" AS PART OF "STRUCTURAL LIBERALISM"

Why are colleges hotbeds of political or cultural liberalism? That's easy. The political left fled to academia, and it has built an empire of like-minded individuals at every university *because* of the structure I have outlined here. It is the structure of elitism and liberalism to which my book points, not the obvious outcome.

If you walk into the offices of the National Organization of Women (NOW) to find a job, you can expect them to hire a pro-choice liberal. If you walk into the Heritage Foundation, you can expect they will hire a free-market conservative. If the faculty of a university is liberal, you can expect they will hire liberals. And, to be fair and honest, where those outposts of conservatism or libertarianism exist, such as at Mason Law, you can expect that the faculty there will hire like-minded people. It is a function of structural liberalism.

Hiring like-minded, political, or philosophical friends isn't news among the university set. Not surprisingly, those friends bring their views, philosophy, ideology, and perspective to our classrooms. As a result, we have the proliferation of a one-side ideology that permeates most institutions. Because of the enormous span and scope of political liberalism on college campuses, we are seeing a few fascinating and troubling realities emerge.

First, while students have access to more information than ever before, they seemingly know less. This is because they are not getting a diversity of opinion, nor are they often being exposed to other views in a productive manner. Conservative ideology doesn't exist on most campuses, and as such, some college kids never hear it or analyze it using critical thinking skills. When professors in some institutions discuss conservatism, they do so in a way that leaves impressionable minds to think political conservatism is dangerous.

In fact, these like-minded factories of political ideology don't use conservative thought for analytical comparison, they often use it for ridicule. The deleterious effects of such like-mindedness should be self-evident, and we see those effects on college campuses where the students live at the intersection of indoctrination, intolerance, political ignorance, and raging hormones.

Ironically, as structural liberalism creates and feeds cultural or political liberalism and political liberalism reinforces structural liberalism, the effect is an even more intolerant society, ill-equipped for diverse views in the marketplace, but deeper in debt. Borrowing 50, 100, or 150 thousand dollars is a lot of money to spend to learn to be like-minded and intolerant.

In a chapter on reforms, I will talk about tenure reform and deregulation requirements that will help undo the structural liberalism. Once campuses are diverse in opinion and running more efficiently to serve the customer, we will see better thinkers, more prepared for the marketplace, and more tolerant of diverse views and philosophy. Reform, however, can't happen without federal, state, and institutional buy-in. Right now, these institutions are run by people with no interest in reform, let alone revolution.

Deans, presidents, and senior management teams of universities are by-products of the structural liberalism of the education industry. If you are picking roommates in NYC, like-mindedness might make a lot of sense. If you are building institutions of higher learning, it is a recipe for intellectual and economic disaster.

Chapter 6

The Rise of the Administrative Machine

WHOSE FAULT IS ADMINISTRATIVE BLOAT?

Colleges are busting out with administrators and administrative staff. Some causes for this are obvious, and others are more controversial. As more kids flood into colleges, these institutions really do need administrative help. No one can deny that.

> The number of non-academic administrative and professional employees at U.S. colleges and universities has more than doubled in the last 25 years, vastly outpacing the growth in the number of students or faculty, according to an analysis of federal figures.[1]

This growth in administrative staff has numerous causes. However, one must ask the simple question: Why are so many resources being pumped into nonacademic, nonteaching roles at our universities? Indeed, with faculties so self-interested, and resources increasingly fewer from state subsidies, why are these dollars being spent this way in public and private schools?

The answer, briefly, is you. Yes, you.

Structural liberalism certainly plays a huge role in the growth of costs at universities. Cultural liberalism, however, also plays an insidious role in driving those costs. When you are a dean at top-tier law school, and a student wants to bring his mom to an informal meeting, you have an anecdotal explanation of a much larger problem. More kids are pouring into colleges, and fewer and fewer of them have the independence of prior college generations.

The helicopter parent has created a dependency, and that dependency requires an army of hand-holders. Moreover, college used to be a means to an end—the primary role was education, and the secondary role might have been

relationship and network building. Colleges now function as social labora-
tories, and they compete to attract students with amenities that include social
planning, events, and magnificent facilities. When they do, they need to hire
all the people necessary to run, promote, and help the students at every turn.

Not all changes and additions are bad, of course. For example, if an institution wants to innovate and offer social services that attract customers, why
shouldn't it? Still, it is the growth of what some call the department of "health
and human services" at schools that is in many ways pushing the number of
administrators to record numbers. Most schools call these departments "student services." Wow, do these services grow every year!

These student services range from organizing socials to helping students
cope with the pressures of school. The rise in some of these services should
be expected, and intervention by psychological services is a welcome addition on campuses. However, if your student services are creating posters to
demonstrate how to put on a condom, one must wonder if that is a role for
higher education.[2]

Likewise, the growth of the number of majors and programs comes with it
an army of advisors, placement professionals, secretaries, buildings, IT infrastructure, security, facilities personnel, and a host of other support roles, all
run by administrators and their burgeoning staffs. Needless to say, one additional cost of the tenure tax is that whatever additional work is required by
adding more and more lifetime faculty also increases the need for more and
more support staff. Plus, faculty simply are not and do not pick up any of the
administrative excess. That becomes a cost pushed onto the university, and
ultimately into your tuition bill.

Not all staff at universities are well paid, but the people who run those
staffs are very well paid and the clear majority of them should be.[3] However,
with each employee at a university comes a strong salary and an outstanding
package of benefits, which include the spiraling cost of health insurance. So,
again, we see an exponential effect on total costs.

This drive to expand programs of study and to create services for kids
when their moms and dads can't be there to help them has a real cost in every
tuition bill. Moreover, what research is showing is that institutions are in an
"amenities arms race" to attract students.[4] As the *Forbes* piece below notes,
rather cryptically, institutions like Harvard don't need to attract students, but
many others do.[5] In fact, read this a few times:

"We found that the lower ability students and higher income students have a
greater willingness to pay for these amenities," says Brian Jacob, a researcher
from the University of Michigan. "The more academic, high achieving students
cared about intellectual achievement."[6]

In unabashed layman's terms, this means that academically strong kids looking for a first-class education don't need or want these services. Likewise, these amenities are not necessary to attract them to an institution.

Whether these are good investments for an individual college or not depends on the success of attracting high-quality students and growing an academic reputation. However, that "success" still sees the cost passed on to the entire student body. For those without a college fund, which is most Americans, these amenities wars are passing on "amenities" costs as educational debt. As we will discuss later, lower-income, lower-academic-performing kids ought to be evaluating both if they should go to college, and if so where.

While it may certainly be true that high-income families of low-performing kids are fueling the amenities arms race, as are parents who have raised more dependent children, universities of every type are also funding and fueling themselves with subsidized debt from a government that encourages students to take on enormous amounts of debt to attend college.

With each amenity and service, each building, and every new major—of any quality—come additional administrative costs. The bloat in administration is real, but it is the result of both structural and cultural liberalism. Structural liberalism is creating programs, majors, and faculties of a dubious nature that never go away. Cultural liberalism is sending kids to school who need more help, more hand-holding, or simply must have certain comforts in order to learn. None of it is a free or cheap to those shouldering the debt.

Chapter 7

Cronyism and the Entitlement of the Lords

"I believe that cronyism is nothing more than welfare for the rich and powerful, and should be abolished."

—Charles Koch

Historical / Academic Underpinnings

Cronyism is a relatively new term

- Traditionally, *corruption* was the primary form of cronyism that concerned political scientists, economists, and journalists
- But corruption is merely one extreme variant (or by-product) of cronyism
- We tried to address on type of cronyism in the 19th century where government jobs were given to family members and friends through the Pendleton Act.
- Political scientists and economists have a long history of critiquing cronyism by other names...

MERCATUS CENTER
George Mason University
4

Figure 7.1.
https://www.slideshare.net/Mercatus/cronyism-history-costs-case-studies-solutions-15163034.

A university solely hiring politically and philosophically like-minded scholars and professors is certainly a problem both economically and educationally. An offshoot of that practice, less pervasive but still damaging and every bit as real and costly in higher education, is the practice of cronyism. People think of modern cronyism as "crony capitalism." That practice of politicians and political parties using friendships, relationships, and lobbyists to pick winners who will receive favorable treatment in bills, contracting, or subsidies, is high on the radar of many Americans. It should be.

This chapter focuses on the more traditional practice of cronyism whereby bureaucratic actors use their position and power to find jobs for friends and relatives. It's a much bigger problem in higher education than most understand. The reason for this is less diabolical than my chapter title may indicate and more a function of the rise of the entitlement culture that structural liberalism creates among the tenured class. It is the power of the Lords in action.

In short, among the self-serving, the idea that a certain class of employees who are highly compensated, underworked, elite, and essentially answer to no one, should have the additional benefit of padding jobs with friends and family, is not outrageous. Why would it be? Structural liberalism creates this entitlement, and helping friends win great jobs by end-running competitive, open hiring practices is not very controversial. After all, higher education has become about them not the educational consumer or Serf.

Ironically, many universities have strict policies against the practice of traditional cronyism. In public universities like George Mason, the policy is to disfavor strongly the practice of cronyism and the even more problematic practice of nepotism. In addition, even if a university grants a waiver in unique circumstances to permit hiring a family member, it requires that a spouse or relative working in the university not report to his or her spouse or relative.

Not having one's spouse report to you as a dean seems like a sensible policy for the spouse, the dean, and all senior staff and employees. In fact, not having one's spouse in the chain of command, reporting up vertically to a spouse, is a good policy. It is particularly sound policy because a spouse reporting up to a spouse, while others must report up vertically to or through that same spouse, is the very recipe for trouble that anti-nepotism policies seek to combat.

Policies that prevent this type of nepotism are made more sound when universities follow them. In fact, one reason good public policy disfavors cronyism and nepotism is because people have a hard time following the rules and ultimately separating the treatment of those hired by powerful friends or family from other employees.

Some might ask, is university cronyism really a high cost to students? That's a fair question. In fact, the more lucid, related question is, "Don't people hired through these types of relationships often fill jobs that would otherwise exist?" They often do. So does cronyism really extract costs on higher education? It does. Let's see how.

Before this chapter takes flight, it is imperative to understand why we are examining this issue. The proposition of this book is that permanent, tenured professors are using these institutions to serve themselves first. That's often true, and it's bad. When they serve the interest of colleagues second, that's bad too. But when students fall behind family colleagues and members, you see an entitlement system that is foisting debt on a class of individuals—the students—whose needs and interests are not even in the top three among stakeholders.

This chapter unbuckles and exposes this entitlement mentality and the accepted practices of the tenure class with a series of examples that lay bare the fundamental problems with cronyism and nepotism in higher education. To do so, the book provides again some real examples of this far too regular practice. The book stakes out the position that nepotism and cronyism are controversial and problematic, which the readers may find a simplistic and obvious conclusion. That's the irony. The tenure class doesn't even recognize the issue, and for those paying the bills—our educational consumers—they may not fully understand how this troubling practice really costs them.

This analysis concedes that to those living life inside the self-interested bubble of higher education and cultural liberalism, these practices are far more acceptable. Again, nepotism and cronyism are, from the insider perspective, an entitlement of the Lords. Those feeding off the system simply don't find the offense of personal profiteering as great as those paying into the system. Perhaps this recitation of facts and analysis will change those views.

The book analyzes this tough topic because of both the direct and indirect traceable costs that ultimately become an additional expense to the far less privileged and entitled tuition payer, whose 30 years of debt are the price of such entitlement. To the extent this book has used prior anecdotal examples, like cars, TVs, Walkmans, and so on, they were used to provide concrete examples that fold more elegantly into a tool of analysis onto which the reader can easily grasp.

To make the point about the corrosive and costly effect of cronyism, the book again examines actual examples of the cronyism and nepotism that show how these costs come to be, why they can mount, and how cronyism hurts morale, pocketbooks, and ultimately credibility. So we will examine real people, real cronyism, and real nepotism.[1]

These revelations are not to titillate, indict, or for retaliatory purposes. They are to educate. The problem of cronyism in higher education is quite profound because of its acceptance, if not the expectation of the practice, irrespective of university policies. As this chapter shows, nepotism and cronyism result in higher costs, lower morale, hidden operational costs, turnover, reten-tion issues, and lost opportunity costs. Indeed, in the case of Mason, cronyism also results in the redirection of university resources and priorities toward a dubious field of study, all of which exacts a cost on the educational consumer *and* the institution.

Remember, having professional relationships is good. Giving recommendations to hiring authorities to interview strong, qualified candidates for a job is also good. Most professionals have hired people and made recommendations about hiring based on relationships and personal knowledge. It is always good to have the recommendation of someone whose judgment you trust and who can vouch for the work, the ethics, and the pro-fessionalism of a candidate. That is not cronyism.

What's cronyism?

You are the newly appointed dean of a law school. You have an opening for a director of development (fundraising). In fact, by every calculable measure, you need to build an entire development office, something in which your institution never previously invested. If this sounds like you, then you could be Henry Butler, the tenured faculty member, and still relatively new dean of Mason Law.

Butler, through a substantially predetermined dean search process, landed the job as Mason Law's new dean, succeeding Dean Daniel Polsby. The faculty chose Henry Butler, one of its own, and that choice then went to the provost and president for approval. The provost and president signed off on the faculty choice of its own member and Mason entered the Butler era.[2] Around April of 2015, Butler got the news of his appointment, with his term beginning by the end of the fiscal year in June. He began his transition immediately and was effectively in charge the day his five-year term was announced.

There may never have been a more consequential deanship appointment to a law school, and only time will tell what those consequences will be. By any measure, even as an insider's pick, Henry Butler had all the qualifications for the position. In fact, among the finalists, objectively, his fundraising credentials made him a frontrunner. Within nine short months, Butler landed a huge gift, changed the name of the school, rebranded a top-tier law school, became embroiled in a national public relations debacle, and he began a much-needed physical-plant renovation project.

Prior to becoming the dean at Mason Law, Butler came home to Mason from Northwestern University in 2010. It was a smart move to recruit Butler to the faculty in 2010 given the money he raised and the synergy his appointment would create with Mason's Law and Economics Center (the "LEC"). In return, Butler landed a great incentive-laden deal. The likely unwritten part of his deal included bringing his spouse into a high-paying role, something common in higher education.

Ironically, at the time of his return in 2010, one assistant dean raised a red flag about hiring his spouse. It wasn't really so much about "his" spouse, but about the complexities of hiring spouses. That dean noted that the deal including Butler's spouse was fresh on the heels of a recent problem from a prior hiring. Mason previously hired a high-profile, high-maintenance law professor who wanted to bring along a spouse and place her in a job. It ended in a contentious and expensive federal lawsuit. The university spent a fortune defending that suit. In fact, some ninth-rate writer wrote a book about it while the suit was ongoing, titled *Truth Be Told*.

The book was worse than the merits of the suit. Still, that university-sanctioned nepotism forced Mason to spend money and resources on defending the action. Fresh from that cronyism/nepotism event, one sensible assistant dean at least raised the issue that bringing in another high-profile law professor and opening a high-paying job for his wife might not be a great idea. Ultimately, Mason decided that acquiring Butler and his likely access to better fundraising was too valuable an opportunity for the institution to pass up, irrespective of any possible ramifications of the Butler/wife issue. Was Mason right or wrong?

Butler was too valuable to Mason economically for it to enforce its own rules on nepotism, and the decision was too easy for a cash-starved law school to pass up. Some felt this deal bringing Butler back in 2010 ultimately would lead to Butler rising to the deanship, though then Dean Polsby seemed skeptical of the suggestion, given Butler's creative, incentive-driven contract as the LEC director. Senior staff, however, were certain Henry Butler was going to be the dean someday, and with him immediately was going to come Mrs. Butler. They were correct.

Henry Butler ran a center at Northwestern University focusing on law and economics as well as other justice reform issues. Merging his center with Mason's LEC brought many opportunities for George Mason. With Henry came support from donors who wanted market-based and justice reform programs that served their agenda and fit into the existing academic tilt of the LEC.

So Henry came to George Mason and took over the LEC. He raised lots of money, and his wife, a capable professional, took a job in the LEC. She was paid quite handsomely too. By university rule, she didn't work for Henry in the LEC. She had a direct report to someone else. In terms of an acquisition, Mason seemingly did quite well. It cut a deal to get a high-value asset. Mason knew that the cost of that "get" wasn't just his incentive-laden contract, but also a high-dollar job for Mrs. Butler. Everyone was happy in 2010, and indeed those who made that deal may still be happy in 2018.

Fast forward from Henry Butler's summer 2010 return to Mason Law to the spring of 2014. Dean Polsby prepared to step back from the deanship and Mason Law entered a "dean search" phase. The law faculty already knew who it was hiring. Butler's LEC was funding substantial portions of the faculty's summer research budget. "Cash is king," Henry Butler tells his team. However, an "official" dean search was necessary, and so Henry Butler increased his visibility at school and student events.

Butler somehow earned the pick as dean in a process that was designed to select him. On the very first day of his first senior staff meeting in July of 2015, a strange thing happened. Mrs. Butler was in the room, handing out an agenda and running the meeting. It was jarring, particularly to a series of senior deans who had pretty much built the law school over 15 to 20 years.

Mrs. Butler had been squirreled away in her LEC job for years. Now all of a sudden, she was Hillary Clinton in 1993 taking over healthcare reform. It's one thing to hire her into the center and pay her more than every single senior dean in the building; it is quite another to have her run the new dean's meetings when she had no such university role. Cronyism had just gone nuclear in the building.

Dean Polsby had already indicated prior to the Butler hire that a change in personnel was coming. I'm not sure even he saw this. Butler did not like anyone casting a shadow on him, and his dean footprint would require, as it should, his team doing things his way.[3] Mason would have been foolish with such a consequential pick not to give the dean a broad discretion to build his team, his way. That is a proper practice in any industry. A Lord, newly appointed by the king, should have his pick of his own loyal knights. Butler's picks certainly tested the bounds of broad discretion.

When Butler joined Mason Law in 2010, he was really coming home. Butler had been a professor and associate dean at Mason Law previously, and part of its complete rebranding in the 1980s. Butler applied to Mason as a junior professor in the 1980s. He was not offered a job at that time. As his good fortune would have it, Mason changed deans and hired one of the fathers of the law and economics movement, Dean Henry Manne. Manne's first hire was Henry Butler, who had studied previously under him in Miami. The two became known as big Henry and little Henry.

Butler, in turn, became the associate dean, and one of his principal jobs was to help recruit law and economics professors and to persuade many existing faculty under the regimes to seek other opportunities. Manne wanted his own people, all professors working in the field of law and economics. At that time, only accredited for a short period, the power of the dean to exert that pressure was quite strong, particularly given the gravitas of Dean Manne taking over a little-regarded institution.

Now, Butler was the dean and he knew how to play the cards better than his mentor. With a bit more history, one would know that Dean Manne fundamentally changed the course and trajectory of Mason Law. Ultimately, however, his authoritarian style led to clashes with students, a public battle with his own Law Review,[4] and an uprising by the very faculty he helped to recruit. That faculty eventually played a role in forcing him out (faculty run the show). The young Henry Butler left too, having failed to win a congressional seat in the 1992 election.

It's 2010, and Butler is back now. After university hopping and building a reputation for successful fundraising, he knew how to spread money, buy influence, and play the politics of higher education. He also knew changing staff could be done by applying pressure first, before having to drop a hammer. Henry was determined to make those changes.

It's August of 2015, and Mason Law has another senior staff meeting. In this one, like the others, Mrs. Butler is questioning senior staff about everything. Having had little relevant experience, she is making suggestions for changes that had been tried previously. The room was literally filled with people who took Mason from the third tier to the first tier with no money. But Mrs. Butler had lots of ideas, and she was likewise certain no one there had thought of them before her arrival.

In one meeting, she openly argued with Mason's finance director. She wanted someone hired, and she didn't rightly care what the HR rules were. Moreover, she didn't want to hear about those rules, even from the only person who did that job for 20 years. She said, "Don't worry about Linda Harber; we know how to get what we want out of her." That turned a few heads among senior staff, as Linda Harber was a university VP and the head of HR for the entire university, of which the law school is about 4 percent of the annual budget.

Mrs. Butler is a talented woman. She simply should not have been in that meeting. She should not have been speaking about anything to senior staff, let alone suggesting that she had any role in hiring or could influence and get her way from the head of university HR. This is why nepotism and cronyism are bad. Again, if one doesn't see events live and witness them, criticizing how a university works sounds more like complaining and theorizing.

Now, watch how Mason worked on this. In September of 2015, just 2.5 months after Henry took over, he sent out an announcement naming Mason Law's new director of marketing. Her name—Mrs. Paige Butler. You can't make that up. By January of that year, he had referred to her in a law community–wide e-mail as "Mrs. Dean Butler."

The position to which Mrs. Butler was appointed would normally be filled through the state's job-search process. Mason is a state university, and the commonwealth has a host of requirements to hire all kinds of positions. Like the federal government, a university also has exceptions to those rigid rules. Deans do have a power of direct appointment. It is strongly disfavored, and it is designed to fill a critical role quickly, with a person whose credentials and experience are beyond reproach. Deans don't like to use these appointments frivolously, and the HR department doesn't like to grant them.

Henry Butler hired his wife as the director of development at Mason Law and used his direct appointment powers to do so. Does that appear bad or hinky? Mrs. Butler certainly played a fundraising role for the LEC, and again, she is a person of marketable talent and skills. It's not that she is unqualified, it is that the university and the dean never bothered to see if someone else might have been better qualified, at a better price point. That doesn't even touch and concern the seemingly obvious issue of the appearance of the appointment. In the legal world, particularly among people who have represented clients and practiced real law, the gold standard of the legal profession, often lost, is that lawyers ought to avoid even the appearance of impropriety.

Butler then paid his wife nearly $80K more than the last person who held the job, a professional fundraiser who raised Mason's participation giving rate among alumni with great success. Butler's wife was now again making more than all the senior staff and many of Mason's professors, including long-serving, prominent, tenured law professors. She then moved into the dean's suite.

That's cronyism wrapped in nepotism. That's still not even close to all the issues, in one department, of one school, in one university. Lest you think the book is picking on the dean or his wife alone, it is not. Other appointments, again, demonstrate how these insider choices of the Lords appear self-serving and indeed appear to place the needs and wants of the entitled class before the tuition payers.

Henry Butler created a new position of senior associate dean and hired his 1992 campaign advisor to fill it. The gentleman, David Rehr, never went to law school. Now, many faculties, including Mason's, hire faculty members from other disciplines to complement the work of their faculty. Indeed, one might argue that Mason's multidisciplinary law faculty is a leader among most law schools, to the extent that is important. The difference in the Butler hire and other historical, Mason Law, non-JD hires for the faculty is that Butler's friend didn't have a law degree, was not a legal scholar, and had not been writing or producing scholarship in support of legal scholars. That's unusual.

He was hired as a term professor at $150,000, and then had to "interview" for the new position of senior associate dean, paying him an additional $35,000. Of course, Mr. Rehr was an affable and pleasant man with some interesting marketing ideas. In addition, he had a PhD in economics from Mason, and he had strong lobbying contacts from prior experience. He might have made a fine marketing officer or communications director, given his experience.

Instead, he was first hired as a consultant to help Butler with his transition. That certainly didn't seem out of the norm given the man's skill set, his familiarity with the dean, and the dean's legitimate need to ramp up transition operations given the tight calendar created by his late appointment. Then Butler hired him as a law professor. That was more than a stretch. After taking over as dean and during that early Butler transition, Mr. Rehr played *de facto* chief of staff with Butler's wife. By the beginning of 2016, senior deans were setting up a hiring process to interview the man for whom they were already working, and to hire him for a senior dean title above their own. Think about that.

Let me explain more deeply how this form of insidious cronyism works and how a public university ignores the letter, spirit, and intention of the law and its own policies to create a hiring opportunity, job, and salary that otherwise would not exist. To be fair, the Butlers didn't invent this work-around. Agencies have been doing this type of hiring for years, though rarely for such brazen cronyism.

Mr. Rehr could not simply be hired as an assistant dean. He could not be hired in any existing dean title. If he were, he would have to be paid the same as the existing deans holding those titles. Butler wanted to pay him more but didn't want to create an equal-pay issue under state law. That is, if he hired Mr. Rehr as an assistant or associate dean at $185,000 a year, he would have to raise the lagging salaries of all the other existing deans.

So Mason hired him as a "term" professor and then interviewed him for a newly made-up, part-time title of "senior associate dean." Under that title, he would be paid more money over and above his "professor" salary. He would then function as the senior dean or chief of staff and make more money than any other dean who had been there for 20 years or more.

The job title and description had to go through the state process since the new dean just burned his direct appointment power on hiring his wife. The job was written such that essentially only internal candidates could apply, and no existing dean would apply over the dean's choice. Talk about a rigged system in a state hiring process, this was it. This was cronyism with a cherry on top. You have a manipulation of state hiring rules, the creation of a new title, the appointment of a professor of law who knows little law, and the manipulation of salary to circumvent pay equity rules. Then you have all the energy and time needed to create such a fiction.

Mrs. Butler was right, they knew how to get what they wanted out of HR. Henry Butler filled two jobs at a total cost of nearly $500,000 annually with benefits. The school had been paying two people to do those jobs for half that, and at one point one of those people was doing both jobs for a quarter of that. The two hires were his wife and his longtime friend and political advisor.

Mr. Rehr had no substantive experience as a law school academic administrator, and he would have no way of knowing or understanding all the various issues, problems, rules, accreditation, and other matters with which a long-serving law administrator might have had experience. But he was the dean's guy, and the dean's guy gets the job and gets paid. The Serfs pay.

Mr. Rehr's first act was to have his office wired for cable so that he could install his TV in the office. Somehow, Mason Law had risen to the top tier of the *US News* law-school rankings faster than any other law school in history without its junior deans being wired for cable. How many David Rehrs do you think are out there in academia?

In a little over a year, Rehr left his duties as the senior associate dean. It apparently didn't work out. He is still there, however, as a "law professor." To replace him, the dean had to promote someone from within the organization and give that dean a substantial and indeed well-deserved raise. Of course, *that dean*, along with others, would have normally been at the front of the line for that position were cronyism not in play.

This type of behavior may not exist in every department of every university, or even in every university. It does, however, exist. It is more prevalent than we know, and it exacts a high cost. Those costs include hard dollars paid to people who ought not have such jobs, as well as the need to pay others to help the unqualified. Or, as in this case, the costs ultimately include those costs necessary to replace the un- or underqualified.

Cronyism destroys productivity. It undermines confidence and it breeds resentment. At Mason, the law school's finance director packed it in.[5] Remember the guy who was arguing with the dean's wife over HR issues before she sternly let him know the dean and she could make the university do what it wants? He left. He served Mason Law in that position for decades. He was invaluable, and he understood not only the school's books and finances, but every component of university procedures and procurement.

Mason went into the open market trying to find a replacement whose knowledge and experience will pale in comparison to the prior director. This will result in innumerable problems with payments, efficiency, and the like. Ultimately, the higher cost of overpaid, underqualified cronies gets passed on to the tuition payer. On the margins, you might say, well, that's not a lot of money. Maybe, but when you look at the ripple effect that causes people to leave, loss of production, additional hires, and ransom holdups by other employees, cronyism costs a great deal.

Finally, to drive this point home on cronyism, it is instructive to review one more critical set of facts. You might be asking yourself, "Wow, why didn't anyone do anything about all this at Mason Law?" Indeed, some people really wanted to step forward, but they knew that they too would be on the firing line. Realistically, this newly approved dean with the high-octane fundraising skills was going to be given a wide berth by the cash-starved university that needed his salve.

In the end, the governor's appointees to the board of visitors must intercede on these issues if the university administration does not. Some of the examples shared here would never have reach the university president. In fairness to him, he would have had no way of knowing of Mrs. Butler's conduct or her declaration that she and her husband could essentially get what they want from the university.

Who in the law school is going to call the university president to say, "Hey, the wife of the new dean you appointed is essentially running the law school." No one is going to do that. Moreover, no one who matters is going to do that. If the faculty is unaffected, no one with enough power could do that.

This type of cronyism and bad behavior does not affect the faculty. In the end, the faculty runs that house, and if they are happy, nothing else matters. Its members are getting their research money. All the people affected by this are at-will employees, including senior staff. If they complain, they will be the first to lose their jobs. Of course, the only other people affected by the acts of the Lords are the tuition payers—the Serfs. We know where they stand in this equation.

The entire cronyism problem at Mason is bigger than just one power-wielding dean and his enthusiastic wife. Cronyism and nepotism are systemic and troubling. What you need to understand about academic cronyism and nepotism is that it is routine, and therefore less jarring, inside the academy than it is outside of the academy. It is part of the self-serving culture.

You might read about these issues and wonder, how do they get away with it? Where are the safeguards? Well, those safeguards got discarded when the president of the same university came to the school and brought his wife into a high-dollar job with him. An "academic" in her own right, President Cabrera's wife stepped into Mason and headed up its university shift toward being a "well-being university."

Perhaps the world is crying out with demand for jobs in the well-being sector? It's not.

This is at best a frivolous field of study that ought to be consigned to private institutions where wealthy parents can afford the cost of such experimentation without regard to value. At worst, it is a prime example of dubious fields of academic study that cost great money and whose subsidies are paid by the tuition of students trying to earn a real degree.

When George Mason University hired Dr. Angel Cabrera from the little-known business school Thunderbolt, President Cabrera brought with him his wife. The university then repurposed an existing center and built in it programming and a focus around "well-being." The president's wife is the Senior Scholar at the "Center for the Advancement of Well-Being at George Mason University." Well-being is in the family at George Mason.

When Henry Butler was negotiating his deal with Dr. Cabrera, who desperately needed a successful fundraiser, it is nearly certain President Cabrera didn't say, "Hey, look, your wife can't have a high-profile job." That would have been awkward.

Whatever are the relative merits of a well-being university we can leave to academics to discuss. Mason, however, only is one because the president's wife is a scholar in the field. Is that a way to make higher education priorities? Every Mason tuition payer and student loan holder is subsidizing that arrangement, as well as all the resources and personnel necessary to create the center, support it, market it, and make sure it is a success. In addition, whatever better use of those resources the university might have had, they are lost forever. That is the price of cronyism, and it is in your bill. Until we find a set of reforms in higher education that truthfully attacks a practice like this, tuition payers will absorb the real costs and the real lost opportunity costs.

The probing question for parents and students looking at a university isn't whether they are going to pay a tax for tenure, inefficiency, and cronyism. The questions are, how high will the tax be, and will it be disclosed? *Mason's problems are not unique.* They are likely not outliers either. That's the point of the chapter. The book could tell you cronyism is bad and that it exists out there in theory. Here, however, you see it in practice.

The irony of these examples is that Mason Law is a considered a conservative law school. It was conservative before it changed its name to Scalia Law. It certainly was conservative before Henry Butler arrived. Indeed, Butler is probably less conservative than the prior dean, who was both a true academic and thoughtful libertarian.

That is important to note because this book deals with "structural liberalism" and not just modern "political liberalism." The full embrace of structural liberalism by the academy includes places like Mason Law, where professors may write and lecture on free markets, the evil of the administrative state, and the need for competition, but they enjoy all the benefits of tenure, cronyism, inefficiency, and the absence of economic incentives and market accountability.

Chapter 8

Is Private Money Donated to Public Institutions Always Good?

ARE THERE HIDDEN COSTS TO "GIFTS"?

Private money has always been in public education. That's generally a good thing. Donations, endowments, and an enduring commitment to an educated populace are essential to a functioning, representative democracy. People who can think and reason are essential for a civil society. Whether money in public education is public or private, how the money is used, who is giving it, and the purpose behind the gift becomes a public concern.

To analyze how education costs continue to spiral out of control, we must look at private giving. Philanthropy ought not to be controversial. That is to say, people giving large sums of money to higher education as charity should be a good thing, right? In this chapter, we examine how private giving may influence what is taught, and by whom. In addition, we will look at how some gifts actually cost universities more money in the long run.

Public universities are scouring the earth for money, now more than ever. There are many reasons for that, but none more glaringly obvious than the structural flaws in the system that prevent efficiency and reordering of priorities and staff. Most public universities are seeing their state support diminish as a percentage of their total budget. Indeed, public university presidents and boards often lament a drop in state support, citing impressive graphs and scary figures to suggest that states simply don't support higher education like they use to do. Not surprisingly, this argument is mostly false and deliberately misleading.

States are still supporting public education quite aggressively, and smart states are doing all they can to buttress public education. The primary function of investment in higher education is to both produce an educated populace in one's own state, and if possible, attract the talent of other states.

Educators know that most students who attended a public university will often settle and work in the local markets tied to that university. That's great for the state's economy, and thus a fine investment.

However, public university budgets have exploded over the last 30 years, and while states continue to invest heavily, the percentage contributed to these schools is lower because these institutions have poor cost controls.

Public institutions have a permanent class of employees who, while highly trained and skilled, are not subject to downsizing. In short, when universities can't downsize, or refuse to look at programs for elimination, or to simply shed programs of little value, costs spiral. States are still investing in public education. The problem is that public education is unaccountable for its costs, performance, efficiency, and production. Thus, the need for resources becomes insatiable.

Universities then must have federal grants, federal research money, cheap federal loans, more students, centers, think tanks, and private money. All of this is to feed a beast that will not be satiated. Research, scholarship, think tanks, and even the most left-fielded areas of study have some intrinsic value. However, many of these endeavors come with personnel costs that become a tax on students. Indeed, the permanent employees in most institutions represent the *tenure tax.*

Instead of narrowing areas of study at public institutions to feed market needs with subjects that provide salable skills, many public universities grow for the sake of growth. The primary beneficiaries of the programs become the permanent employee class and the university administration and administrators who run these institutions. The higher education establishment has never had an honest discussion about right-sizing and prioritizing academic programs.

In 2006, the provost of a university yelled at an alumni president in a private meeting, exclaiming that "[I] would not ever treat academic units differently." What he meant, to be plain, is when he made budgets, all academic units would suffer or profit the same, without respect to value. That guy is still collecting a huge check as a tenured professor. He not only could not see the problem, he had no idea he was part of it.[1]

The alumni president was simply shocked by the provost's seemingly untenable and indefensible position. As one smart dean once said of education funding, "You can keep cutting the oats to all the horses, but eventually they will all starve." That dean was right; at some point, you need to decide how many horses you really need—and what is needed to make them thrive.

This is why the push for private money in higher education has never been stronger. Public institutions remain unwilling to address priorities in higher education. Thus, they simply search for resources, and when they can't find them, they hoist the cost of their poor leadership onto the backs of tuition borrowers. It's a horrible system, fraught with peril. Moreover, it breeds desperation. With desperation comes dubious decision making by administrators that leads to questions from stakeholders about the source of private money, its purpose, and the real strings attached thereto.

Philanthropy is almost never about what a university wants; it is about the wants and desires of the donors. Those desires are dramatically different based on the donor and program. However, it is plainly foolish if one does not admit that most donors give to an institution to exert influence or push an agenda.

In some instances, powerful donors want to buy the right to determine the type of education, the programming, and the philosophy of educators. Money buys influence, and influencing young minds buys power. None of this is bad if everyone knows who is buying what from whom. In addition, if the charity comes without additional costs to the university, then analyzing the purpose is the only consideration for accepting the deal. If, however, the "gift" puts the university on the hook for millions of dollars in the future, such a gift should be subject to additional scrutiny.

In the private university world, this analysis is mostly irrelevant. Where private money comes to influence state universities, already funded by taxpayers, those questions are real—and transparency is essential.

A recent gift to George Mason University provides a great example of how philanthropy can influence the agenda in higher education and how such philanthropy can also drive up long-term costs to a university. While the gift came with interesting political drama, few focused on the "cost" of the gift to the university over time. Looking at the deal closely, the gift certainly provides short-term, much-needed advantages to Mason University. However, due to the tenure tax and the structural liberalism of universities, this right-wing gift could be quite costly to George Mason. In the end, that means it could be quite costly to tuition payers.

The details of the gift broke into the public after the leak of the grant agreement. That leak and the public discussion over the politics of the gift inspired a left-leaning organization to bring suit against George Mason. The organization, Transparent GMU, is represented by an even more far-left organization, called Appalachian Mountain Advocates. These are groups with an obvious political agenda and their concern about such a gift grew from anger that the gift would force on the institution a political agenda with which they disagreed.

As honest brokers in a functioning civil society, however, it is incumbent upon us to look at the merit of the complaint, and not just its political motivation. The primary interest of these groups is not the more important issue of improper private influence of public education. Their issue is the influence of private money on public institutions by people they don't like. Inside their motivation and bias, however, rests a fair question about private money and its influences on public education, irrespective of political bent. Inside of that question lies a subject of this book. What if some charitable giving, shrouded in secrecy, costs a university more money than the gift?

Transparent GMU members belong to radical groups that oppose gifts from conservatives, including and especially the Koch Foundation and the Koch brothers. These left-leaning organizations would not be bringing suit against Mason if George Soros had given the university $30 million. While the suit specifically addresses FOIA rights and the symbiotic relationship between the public university and a private foundation raising money in its name, the bigger point the suit raises is worthy of discussion in the context of the higher education crisis this book examines.

WHERE IS THE LINE ON PRIVATE GIVING AND PUBLIC DISCLOSURE?

George Mason, like nearly every public institution, has a private foundation whose dedicated purpose it is to raise money for the university. The people working in such foundations are highly skilled and dedicated. Most of them are, in the case of Mason, quite literally Mason Patriots.[2] They are true believers in Mason's mission and its critical impact in the Northern Virginia community.

The higher education industry relies on these individuals to find resources to make communities like Mason stronger through philanthropy. Of course, merely hunting revenue is no substitute for a public institution's increasing need to address the issues, priorities, values, efficiency, and the strength and focus of that public university.

However, the foundation's work is not about that. It is committed to locating resources. It is the board of visitors, the president, provost, and deans who ultimately make policy about the direction and use of those resources.

The lawsuit by Transparent GMU filed in early 2017 is an interesting one. It focuses on the intersection of public university and private foundation functions. Nearly everything that happens in a public university is subject to the rule of transparency, including routine e-mails and the like. With private foundations, however, nearly everything they do they may shield from that transparency.

The central question becomes, as set out in the lawsuit, can a public university use a private foundation to hide from the public activities and disclosures that would otherwise be public if not performed for the university by the foundation? It's a fair and important question. To be sure, the ties of any foundation with the university to whom it is dedicated are close.

The driving force behind the Transparent GMU suit may be transparently political. Still, the group wants to know who is giving money to the university, and what promises, if any, the university and its leader are making in return. Moreover, it wants to know who assumes the risk of those promises. Those questions are not inherently political.

At least initially, the lower court has found that Transparent GMU's suit cannot reach foundation documents.[3] Still questions about these relationships and the money and donors they shield are worth consideration.

THE SCALIA NAME CHANGE
DONATION AT MASON LAW

George Mason University was the recipient of a generous pair of gifts, the result of which was a change of the name of the law school. Even if one were a great admirer of Justice Scalia, and the name change was personally pleasing, the strategic decision to make the change, and the way it was done, are issues worthy of closer investigation to determine if the short-term gift is a much more, longer-term expense to the university because of, ironically, structural liberalism.

It is a matter of public record that Mason Law needed the money. It really needed the money. The financial state of Mason Law was very weak prior to this gift. In fact, the publicly available accreditation documents show the debt of the school, the concern of the faculty, and the lack of a long-term commitment by the university to fund the school in a manner necessary to keep it as a first-tier law school.

The donors made a wise and great investment in one of the best institutions in legal education. Indeed, they made a better deal than this book can explain. As this chapter will set out, the donors got a name change and bought 12 professors, support staff, and support for two right-leaning "academic" centers. The money they gave helps Mason in the short run, but it saddles Mason with more than $2.3 million of annual expenses in the out years, after the gift money runs out.

Mason Law and the university would have been fools to reject the donation—*if* it was free from any other strings other than the name change. It is on that point that we start our investigation, with consideration of the aforementioned principles of conflict and transparency.

What the donors wanted, other than to change the name of the institution, is a great question. Not a single person on earth thinks the leaked donation agreement[4] and the unknown $20 million donation were for the purpose of minting new lawyers and providing scholarship funds and operating capital to a law school to do so.

Likewise, while the Koch Foundation likely admires Justice Scalia, it didn't contribute simply to name the building after that fine justice. The school naming was an opportunity for the donors and the school. Who got the best of the deal? Did Mason do well enough on the deal, even if it didn't do the best?

Indeed, the leaked agreement makes plain what the quid was for the money. First, they wanted a dean on whom they could lean and trust. They wanted their man, and they likewise wanted to make sure that a liberal university wouldn't change their man after the deal was cut. They wanted someone they had previously done business with, and who they knew would deliver as requested.

However, the key to the agreement, which absent a leak by a Mason insider never would have been known, is that Mason Law intends to hire 12 more tenure-line faculty members. It requires the school to raise money to fund 12 faculty positions, staff support, and additional support for two right-leaning law centers. That requirement was met with the second anonymous gift procured at the exact same time.

While the grant agreement pays lip service to "academic freedom," it defines the school's mission as law and economics and other such social sciences. In short, the $10 million donation was an integral part in mandating that Mason hire a particular type of professor with a particular type of ideology. The agreement was that a tenured law faculty of 37, with a dwindling student population, hire 12 more of that particular type of law professor.

To be clear, such an agreement is legal, and it may even have merit. However, if a donation is locking a dean in place and securing 12 members of an ideological movement, increasing staff, and building out ideological centers, should it be private in a public university? *It should not.*

If such an agreement is going to leave the institution on the hook to fund these professors, centers, and staff when the donation runs out, shouldn't the public know about it? Should the public be permitted to know and examine everything about *this transaction* and donation to a public institution by a private donor? Common sense says they should.

Donors give for their own reasons; public institutions ought to let the public know what those reasons are, and what the costs and risks of the donation might be. If a university must choose between a private agreement and nondisclosure, versus no donation, keeping an agreement private sure makes sense. However, it's what's inside the agreement that matters most.

Public institutions have boards, presidents, deans, lawyers, and others who are hired to safeguard the public's interest when they make these agreements. That argument is sound, and sensible. However, if the agreements both change the political ideology of an institution, and those making them have an interest, a conflict, or bear no risk for making those agreements, disclosure of the terms is in the public interest.

In the instance of the Scalia agreement, this was NOT merely an agreement to give money to support the school. It was an agreement that put the school on the hook to hire 12 professors. An agreement that binds a public institution to spending money, for decades on end, to support a class of permanent employees, of a distinct ideology, ought not to be protected by nondisclosure.

The functional result of running such an agreement through the foundation is to hide its purpose, and more troubling, to hide its effect. In fact, if one had not spent one's time in the administration at Mason Law, one might be hardpressed to understand what this agreement does.[5]

The Scalia name and the emotionally wrought, silly arguments springing from the name change were a complete diversion in this instance. Left-leaning students and left-leaning academics missed the point. So angry were they with Scalia's name, so amused were they by the foolish acronym and nearly incompetent rollout, that they lost the purchase in the agreement.

The name change surprised many alumni and law professors, and some were upset because of the political and emotional issues. The truth be told, the new dean, Henry Butler, was running a law school that was operating at an unsustainable financial loss, such that without a university subsidy, or outside money, the school would have gone bankrupt before Butler's term ended.

This is not to suggest that the university would have permitted that to happen, but the law school losses, even without the scholarship money needed to keep its numbers up, were very high. How long the university would have funded the law school's losses without cutting the aid necessary to buy good students was unknown.

George Mason already had a series of significant financial issues university-wide, springing from a host of poorly thought out, ill-conceived ventures from the Merten era. Heck, the university was forced to sell its own new hotel it built on Mason property, converting the hotel into a dorm for a cash payment from an entity that places foreign students.

The Scalia name change came about when Mason's law school needed the money most. Upset alumni could not have known the financial reality Butler was facing. He could take $30 million now, or he could raise that $30 million from the alumni. Since law school alumni donations routinely came in around $175,000 a year, Butler would have had to wait 171 years to raise that money. He wasn't going to make it. Making half the alumni unhappy, when only 10 to 12 percent give anything each year, was not a hard choice for a law and econ guy.[6]

Rather than rehash the character of Mr. Butler, this analysis is an honest look at why any dean would have looked for a way to obtain and accept the donation he orchestrated, and why some transactions belong in the bright light of day, just like some hiring decisions and the waivers approving them. The question, however, is, did Butler and the faculty have to commit to hiring 12 professors to get the money? And if they did, does that make economic sense? Moreover, should a public institution have to divulge such conditions?

In short, Butler traded $10 million in grant money for an obligation to hire and fund 12 tenure-line law professors until those professors leave, quit, or die.

Let's look at that trade.

First, the agreement essentially locks Butler in place over the five years. To obtain this initial grant, the university committed to raise another $20 million, which it purportedly did through a companion donation that is "anonymous." One cannot imagine who would make such a donation as a companion donation alongside the Koch Foundation. Hmmm?

Butler made the first deal knowing they had the second gift of $20 million. So, in fairness, we must look at the trade of 12 tenure spots, the employee support, and two centers for both the $10 million in scholarship money and the $20 million in naming money.

The Koch Foundation gets 12 professors. They get their guy Henry Butler to ride the faculty for those hires. Law and economics scholars already dominate the faculty. They present at innumerable conferences funded by like-minded donors, and their faculty summer research dollars were doled out for years by the law and economics center Butler once ran. In short, all the Koch faculty hires will be law and economics/libertarians. Again, many conservative alumni were not unhappy, even if those may not be the school's primary needs.

What do all these new professors cost?

Junior law professors are coming in around $110,000. Midlevel professors come in around $140,000. Senior-level, high-profile professors can range up much higher, but if we chose a low ball of $200,000, that would be more than fair to analyzing the deal.

Henry Butler committed to hiring the following:

6 x $110,000 x .35 for fringe and benefits = $891,000 a year, every year.
3 x $140,000 x .35 for fringe and benefits = $567,000 a year, every year.
3 x $200,000 x .35 for fringe and benefits = $810,000 a year, every year.

Of course, this assumes they never get raises or promotions. The Koch brothers bought $2,265,000 a year in professors, not including support staff and the cost of both centers. The $20 million of additional money raised over the name-change "donation" would pay for about 8 years and 11 months of these new hires. After that, a school that was losing nearly $2 million a year before the gift will be paying for these new professors by itself, on top of the overhead it has right now that it can't afford.

Now, if you get $10 million for scholarships to buy your class, shoring up your rank, that's still a pretty good deal. Cash is king, and cash in hand beats cash in the future. Most Scalia Law competitors have been discounting tuition to manipulate ranks and to continue to attract a dwindling pool of talented law applicants. This chunk of money serves two immediate purposes: it counts as revenue direct to the university, which slows the need for subsidies, and it provides much needed flexibility for Mason admissions to buy down tuition of higher, stronger applicants.

The deal may work out. It's a risk, and it's a bigger risk than most understand. However, taking no money was not an option because of the structure of tenured faculty. In short, the law school's biggest expense could not be cut.

Here's the piece that even savvy observers couldn't possibly know. After losing his 1992 congressional bid, and having his mentor driven out of the Mason deanship shortly thereafter, Henry Butler hit the road for an odyssey that took him to multiple institutions where he built his résumé, raised money, and grew a constituency for conservative donations to centers run by Butler and his wife.

Back at Mason, the faculty, administrators, students, and alumni took a third-tier law school left in shambles by Dean Manne and his associate dean, Henry Butler, and grew it into a first-tier law school. That was all done, Butler-free. In fact, Mason became the law school that reached the top tier of the *US News* rank faster than any other. By the mid-2000s, Mason peaked at 34 in the *US News* ranks, which for better or worse, is the Holy Bible of the legal consumer.

Mason Law did all that on a remarkably skinny budget, often one of the most underfunded law schools in the country. Tuitions were low too. By and large, it had nearly 650 students in the law school with a tenured faculty of 35 to 37, depending on various factors. The university raised tuition regularly, and over a 5- to 6-year period, eliminated Mason Law's competitive price advantage. The excess money from the tuition premium the university pushed on the law school was not reinvested in the law school. The university hauled it out of the first-tier law school and spread it around a third-tier university, which is how the deeply flawed higher education model works.

By 2010, Mason Law reached the confluence of a series of events that threatened its rank and existence. The legal market collapsed, the economy would not recover, innovation and outsourcing strapped legal demand, law school applications began to dry up, and like nearly every law school, applications shrank. As applications shrank, classes shrank. As classes shrank, the student quality numbers, GPA and LSAT, receded.

By 2013, instead of admitting targets of 210 to 215 JD students, Mason Law was admitting only roughly 150 students. Did it cut tenured faculty? Well, now you know the answer to that—it couldn't.

So by the time the university hired Henry Butler as the new law dean, Mason had a total enrollment that was closer to 470 or so students than 650. It had lost nearly 30 percent of its student body. Tuitions were high, and the law school had, relative to its competitors, very little scholarship money to give to a dwindling number of high-caliber candidates.

To make matters worse, during the wine and caviar days of the mid-2000s, the faculty and administration had created an LLM product that no one wanted. Literally, in most years, the program enrolled not one person. The product offered advanced law and economics classes, it had a very high credit-hour requirement, and it was very expensive. The end result was that as regular JD applications fell and prices rose, the law school of free markets kept the same size faculty, and it could not create an LLM product to generate more than a handful of non-JD customers.

Why is this so critical? Because as the JD market collapsed, many schools in strong markets were falling back on revenue from non-JD programs. Mason could not.

Henry Butler set out to find cash, and given his track record of attracting cash for programs, Butler became Mason's primary hope to find outside money. Senior staff didn't know the details, but they were aware that he was working known contacts for some type of investment in Mason Law.

The sudden death of Justice Scalia became an opening. Only the Butlers know the exact manner in how the deal came to be. However, he made a deal that will ultimately cost the university more than $2.3 million a year to support the center and staff and permanent, tenured law professors of the Koch Foundation's choosing. He adds those permanent faculty to the faculty Mason already has, which is way too large for the student body it currently teaches.

The law school has been spending its scholarship cash aggressively, and the result has been a minor uptick in JD applicants, as well as a minor rebound in JD applicant numerical quality. However, the law school needs that number to climb to roughly 200 to 205 students each year just to break even, assuming no massive scholarship buy downs. It's not there, and it's not close ... yet.

So why hire 12 more faculty members?

Butler has made an agreement to expand the tenured faculty at the law school by 32 percent when the student body is down over 30 percent. In that agreement, he agrees to hire a certain type of faculty member. It's audacious, to say the least.

Had the agreement for the name change disclosed these facts, as well as the philosophical requirement, prior to its announcement, Virginia taxpayers and Mason Law stakeholders could have asked some serious questions about the risk involved. Maybe everyone would be forced to agree that it was the best deal, and times were too critical to let the money pass. Maybe, if the university did its job, it would have right-sized other underperforming units and centers and reinvested in its top-tier law school. That's the critical point, isn't it? Good deal or not, Mason was driven to it because structural liberalism would not permit it to decide how to reapportion and right-size its own operation.

For some on the hard left, like the Transparent GMU gang, the deal likely would never have been good enough.

Still, were they wrong to insist that it be transparent?

Right now, Scalia Law has some up-front cash, and it is making good with it on the scholarship front. Likewise, Butler and his team of Mrs. Butler have a plan to upgrade the law building to better attract more students and make the space more law school friendly. That million dollars plus plan is a good one, and well overdue.

The private money deal has immediate winners, some immediate losers, and a great number of unknown risks. The first, immediate winner is Henry Butler. He scored a $30 million gift, and his plan of serving only five years as dean will ensure that the benefits of the cash come through on his watch. Henry Butler and team Butler have done a world-class job of winning, grabbing the benefits, and assigning all risks elsewhere.

The Koch Foundation is an immediate winner. It bought 12 spots on a first-tier law school faculty, support staff, and support of two, right-leaning centers. It paid $10 million over five years for a $2.3 million annual expense that ends only when all its professors die or leave voluntarily. That's a good deal.

Great law applicants interested in a terrific education at the law school with the best physical location in DC are immediate winners. The new Scalia Law has cash, and it will, indeed it must, spend that money aggressively to attract those overqualified applicants. Those applicants drive the rank of the law school, and ultimately, while they may have first-year scholarships, their second- and third-year dollars keep Scalia Law afloat.

The money and its use to attract applicants in the short term should keep Scalia Law in the top tier, and that is an immediate benefit to the university, the law students, and its alumni. For Mason Law graduates of a political bent, of which there are many, the name change became an instant disconnect. Butler and his team wrote those graduates off. While getting the cash now was essential, the cost of the loss of some robust and strong alumni will have long-lasting effects—effects the Butlers won't be worrying about. They have their money and their timeline.

What happens when the money runs out, the faculty is much larger, and the FTE (full time equivalent) or body count does not even rebound to precollapse levels?

In short, what if Butler doesn't get Mason back to 200-plus law students and LLMs annually? Scalia Law will have 30 percent more faculty, over $2.3 million in permanent employees, and it will be burning cash at a record level.

Who takes that risk?

The tenured faculty does not. Its members can't be fired. Indeed, at Mason, if the law school shuttered its doors, the university would have to find spots for law faculty in the university faculty. The Butlers will be living on their farm in happy retirement, so no risk falls to them.

It's the taxpayers and the University alumni who take the risk. If Butler's agreement doesn't work, he bears none of that burden. For a law school that teaches "incentives matter," the risks have all been passed on to a later generation. This long, detailed chapter about one group, one donation, and one institution may seem like an unnecessary deep dive. It is not. It is the inner workings of an institution that is starved for cash and making deals with long-term risk that likely increase the cost of higher education.

So this brings us back to the key question: with private money in public schools, should we have more transparency and more disclosure? Is it always in everyone's interest that a public institution can hide certain types of transactions in private entities that essentially only serve a public function?

The governor, the board of visitors, the president, his staff, and the two main players at the law school, Mr. Butler and Mrs. Butler, vetted this "deal." Maybe that is enough, but not one of them will be around if the deal goes south, and only the taxpayers and future tuition payers will get the bill.

Any private deal that influences the political bent of a public institution, or assigns all the risk to the non-dealmakers, is a deal that ought to be subject to disclosure before it is agreed upon. Given the inability of most universities to run their operations efficiently and effectively in a cost-effective manner for the educational consumer, the deals they make with pros ought not to be made in darkness.

Chapter 9

Revenue Predators

Have Colleges Become Revenue Predators?

IF SO, WHO IS THE PREY?

Greed is good—so famously said the character Gordon Gekko in the classic 1980s movie *Wall Street*. Putting aside the philosophical debate on "greed" and what it is, in higher education we must examine colleges and their race for revenues. As we talked about in chapter 6, colleges are in an amenities war. They are doing whatever they can to attract students. Competition is good. Making schools compete for you is good. However, do we want schools competing for us based on creature comforts or on academic excellence?

In modern America, schools are no longer merely competing for outstanding students, they are angling to attract revenue. Why are they doing this now when tuitions are so high? Schools are chasing students because students are the vehicle for easy money. They are hunting unsuspecting students because that cheap federal money given as subsidized loans spends well, as does the money of upper-middle-class families with substandard students looking for any college degree. The difference between trying to attract great students and hunting revenue is quite stark.

A great university attracts students based on its academic reputation. Schools at the top of the academic food chain have no problem attracting high-quality students and ample applications from other applicants who are either completely or nearly qualified prospects for that institution. Even without their endowments, Duke, UVA, Yale, Stanford, and Harvard, among others, are never going out of business. The competition for students among those institutions is a competition for the best and brightest, for the most part. It is not a hunt for customers and revenue.

Isn't that what colleges should be doing? Shouldn't colleges be investing in quality education and building a first-class reputation, either locally, regionally, or nationally? If not-for-profit colleges and universities were really "not-for-profit," wouldn't the sole factor in investment and recruitment be strong academics and programs designed to raise academic standards and reputation? Make no mistake; it's fine for a university to invest in infrastructure and amenities as part of a strategy to improve its appeal and to attract quality students to its campus—if attracting them is for the purpose of landing great students, rather than merely getting revenue any way it can, just so that it can pay its faculty and administrators.

In many universities, and indeed in some colleges and departments within universities, the fight to attract students is all about what we in administration call FTE. An FTE is a "full-time equivalent" revenue source. A university that spends its time counting FTE instead of thinking about applicants as students is usually a revenue predator. A student is a human being seeking knowledge, an education, and a degree with the imprimatur of the institution he or she attends.

Before choosing a college, you should want to know if you are a valued, high-quality student, or merely revenue to feed the beast. The best way to evaluate whether an institution is a revenue predator is to look at its academic quality ratings, its size, its endowment, and the number of ancillary, nondegree programs it is pushing. Revenue predators may be both "for-profit" or "not-for-profit" institutions. The defining characteristic of a revenue predator isn't profit, it is that they are cash-starved. They have overhead they cannot get rid of, and an entitled class that needs to be paid. Thus, the central focus of their institution isn't academic excellence, it is attracting customers irrespective of academic excellence.

THE NOT-FOR-PROFIT RUSE

One of the great lies of academia today is that traditional, not-for-profit universities are somehow better, more noble, more trustworthy, and less "greedy" than newer for-profit universities. This idea goes back to the concept that greed is bad, profit is bad, and indeed, trying to "profit" off education is bad, wrong, and evil. We see this type of debate and the same suspect arguments advanced with respect to healthcare policy. The idea of some in the cultural left is that "profiting" off healthcare is wrong and immoral.

In reality, a for-profit system is designed to wring out all the inefficiencies we have discussed so far. For-profit systems seek efficiency, innovation, and price competition. Those incentives and structures encourage people to deliver products and services better and cheaper than the competition so that the innovators can profit. The chart on the front of this book is a study in the contrast between deregulated, for-profit industries, and heavily regulated, "not-for-profit" industries.

Not-for-profit status is nothing more than a legal and accounting gimmick. It merely means the entity, at the end of the year, if money is left over, does not take that left-over money as "profit." It does not distribute left-over money or "profits" to owners who have shares. In a university with a billion-dollar budget and thousands of employees, lots of people are profiting, irrespective of the university's status. If a not-for-profit university has revenue at the end of a cycle or fiscal year, it spends it within departments or on projects and personnel.

Tenured professors, presidents, deans, coaches, and all the other employees working at a university are eating out of that revenue, and they need that money. Never confuse "not-for-profit" with the idea of "charity." College professors, presidents, deans, and college coaches make hundreds of thousands of dollars, and indeed some make millions. There is no charity in the not-for-profit higher education industry. There are lots of costs, some of them permanent, as we discussed, and someone must pay the bills. That someone is the tuition payer, primarily.

The greatest misdirection in America today is the idea that the nonprofit higher education industry is working to create a stronger, more educated, prosperous society. It is not. Indeed, in many ways, the not-for-profit or nonprofit institutions are nothing more than revenue predators whose first mission is to draw in customers to feed an army of tenured professors and career administrators.

For certain, not all colleges are revenue predators. There are a handful of U.S. universities whose endowments are so large they could run their institutions on little or no tuition for decades on end, just living off the revenue of the endowments. Not surprisingly, most of these institutions are also high-quality, well-known academic powerhouses that have an endless supply and long line of people willing to pay for the privilege and prestige of attending.

Table 9.1

School name (state)	End of fiscal year 2016 endowment	US News rank
Harvard University (MA)	$35,665,743,000	2
Yale University (CT)	$25,413,149,000	3 (tie)
Stanford University (CA)	$22,398,130,000	5 (tie)
Princeton University (NJ)	$21,703,500,000	1
Massachusetts Institute of Technology	$13,181,515,000	5 (tie)
University of Pennsylvania	$10,715,364,000	8
Texas A&M University—College Station	$9,858,672,136	69 (tie)
University of Michigan—Ann Arbor	$9,600,640,000	28
Columbia University (NY)	$9,041,027,000	5 (tie)
University of Notre Dame (IN)	$8,748,266,000	18 (tie)

** USNEWS 2017 Data[1]

Nine of the ten largest endowments belong to schools universally recognized as top institutions. Seven of them have top 10 *US News* rankings, and two others are ranked inside the top-30 of all colleges. Harvard could spend $1.8 billion a year just off its endowment. Think about that differently. If Harvard donated 5 percent of its university endowment, less than it makes each year in investments, it could fund the largest state university in Virginia, which is George Mason.

Indeed, Mason has over 30,000 students, multiple campuses, and a billion-dollar annual budget. Harvard could fund Mason with the 5 percent revenue from its endowment and Mason would still have nearly $800 million left over, after the donation. Harvard is a nonprofit.

Harvard raises lots of money, but no one gets up every day at Harvard worrying about paying the bills, staying in business, attracting students, or finding revenues. The same cannot be said about the George Masons of the world, or the clear majority of the 5,300 colleges and universities in this country. For those institutions, revenue is an essential part of survival. As costs continue to grow due to structural liberalism, these colleges are out in the market hunting revenue, like predators.

Revenue predators are easy to identify. They have low endowments, and they have more majors and programs than menu items at a New Jersey diner. They also tend to have a mediocre rank. Indeed, in many instances, their ranking is boosted only by one or two departments, while the rest of the larger university is a bit of a drag on the operation. There are innumerable numbers of these revenue predators out there, and you need to make sure you understand what you are buying when you buy into such an institution.

Obviously, there are many tools for ranking universities, and you should be using as many as possible to synthesize those rankings to make a judgment call when choosing where to invest. Assuming, again, you are not going to Harvard or Yale, or that your parents or family are not paying, choosing a college is all about selecting the right major, at the best price, at the best possible institution. A quick look at three Virginia state schools will help you identify a revenue predator.

The University of Virginia is a top-ranked school, and it has a huge endowment. Its endowment is nearly $270,000 per pupil.[2] Christopher Newport is a smaller, much younger university with a strong, fast-emerging reputation and a small, but nearly brand-new, state-of-the-art campus. It has a low per-pupil endowment of $4,882 per student.[3] George Mason University is the largest public university in Virginia, and it has a per-pupil endowment of only $2,659 per student. Its aid to undergraduates is in the bottom 10 percent of all universities, even though its acceptance rate is remarkably high.[4]

Low aid and a high acceptance rate is a red flag, and certainly strong evidence of a revenue predator among four-year intuitions. Indeed, this chart (figure 9.1) was making the rounds at Mason long before a website published it.[5] President Cabrera of George Mason University often gives a presentation to his development team and select audiences on this chart.

This does NOT mean you can't obtain a value degree from George Mason. Indeed, its physical location in a major job market, its regional reputation, and its alumni network are of great aid to prospective graduates. However, Mason is not going to give you much help financially, and if you are not careful about the quality of your major at a school like Mason, you could walk out with a degree in something of little value. When the degree is of little value, it is necessarily overpriced. Mason has many such selections. Don't let Mason, or any institution, pitch you on numbers and stats unrelated to your major.

Taking an economic risk and investing in one's own future is smart, if the investment is smart. Many such investments are not, and the institutions are less concerned about where you will be financially in 10 years than where they will be in their own next budget cycle. When American educational consumers understand this reality, they can begin to make better decisions.

In decades past, a college degree was the symbol and an indicium that a person had a level of education, responsibility, and independence that alone made them a good economic bet for many employers. We are way past that quaint and bygone time. While it is true that a college degree remains the entry requirement for most jobs, merely having a degree, in any subject, does

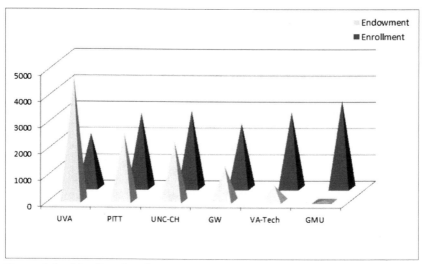

Figure 9.1. http://gmufourthestate.com/2014/03/09/masons-endowment-funds-pale-in-comparison-to-other-virginia-colleges/.

not mean you are sure to be hired. Moreover, with the spiraling cost of a degree, it is often likely that the job you obtain may not be sufficient to justify the paper in which you invested.

It has always mattered, for preference and market purposes, where one gets a degree, in what field, and how well one did. It just simply matters so much more now because the market is flooded with college degrees of suspect quality. Many of these degree programs don't provide skills that are in market demand. In fact, many of these students come out seemingly missing the essential component of any degree—the ability and desire to think critically. That is a result of cultural liberalism.

Meanwhile, American graduates are competing in a global employment market. Put more simply, we have high-end college graduates from around the world competing for jobs in the U.S. market that used to be the exclusive providence of American students. Likewise, multinational corporations can use employees outside the States to fill needs that previously required an employee to live in the United States. The United States has nearly 330 million citizens and residents. India has almost 300 million college graduates. The market for high-quality college graduates is good and getting better for companies, which means it is getting tighter for our graduates.

American universities need to reprioritize how they serve students, and how and why they attract students. They cannot do that until their primary function becomes serving students first and the academic and tenure class second. The education industry must make immediate reforms, and among those reforms must be a strong, comprehensive review of the programs, classes, courses, and majors that universities are pushing on our kids at great cost. We need tenure reform too, as the costs of these programs are reflected in a tenure tax where lifetime employment is the result of fields of study that universities create and feed, but never eliminate or reduce.

Universities hunt for revenue among weak prey, drawing them in under the guise that "every kid must get an education in something." The institutions get the cash, professors get protections, and the kids get the bill in a tenure tax that is breaking us economically and socially.

In part 2 of this book, I will propose reforms to the system and provide a roadmap for students and parents to find and make the best choices for their education. Hints already abound in this book.

Chapter 10

Is That Degree Worth the Debt?

"If you want more of something, subsidize it. If you want less of something, tax it."

—Ronald Reagan

Degrees of Debt & Regret

45%
of people with student loan debt said that college was not worth the cost.

44%
would want to know how much student debt a person has before beginning a serious relationship.

28%
delayed buying a house because of their debt.

12%
delayed marriage because of debt.

Figure 10.1.
From site: https://www.review-mag.com/article/collecting-1-of-student-debt-costs-american-taxpayers-38.

The best way to run up debt is to make money widely available to nearly anyone and do so on strongly favorable terms. Or, in short, give them cheap money and decades to pay it back. If you really want to help people get in debt, get them at eighteen, let them study anything they want, give them a fat loan, and tell them repayment doesn't kick in until after they graduate.

Student loan debt is insane. Americans owe $1.45 trillion in student loans; that's over $600 billion more than credit card debt. The class of 2016 has an average debt of over $37,000.[1] That's before you go to graduate school.

In the last decade, student loan debt is up 62 percent and the number of people with more than $50,000 in student loan debt has tripled in that same period.[2] With tuitions increasing, it is only going to get worse. In fact, in that same period, the value of that degree decreased, and so did the return on it.

It is one thing entirely to invest in one's self and leverage one's debt for higher wages, but we are now seeing a deadly predictor of financial doom. People are incurring more financial debt for higher education while wages have either decreased or remained stagnant.

"Go to college," they said. "You must get an education," they said. "If you don't get a college education you will never go anywhere," they said. The higher education industry is the Fannie Mae and Freddie Mac of our next economic crisis. When the student loan bubble bursts, we will look back at universities and governments and ask, "Who thought it was a good idea to push everyone into college to study subjects that are valueless in the market?"

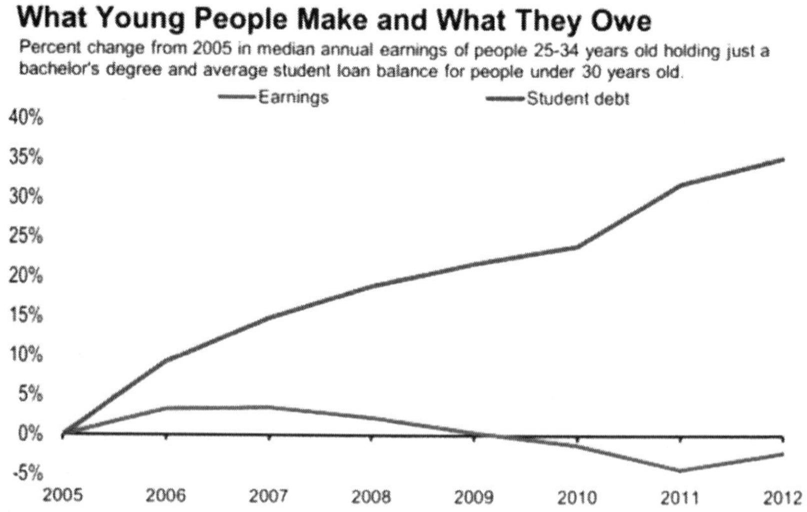
What Young People Make and What They Owe
Percent change from 2005 in median annual earnings of people 25-34 years old holding just a bachelor's degree and average student loan balance for people under 30 years old.
Earnings
Student debt
40%
35%
30%
25%
20%
15%
10%
5%
0%
-5%
2005
2006
2007
2008
2009
2010
2011
2012

Figure 10.2.
https://twitter.com/WSJ/status/467905839815458816.

By education, the industry really means a degree from an accredited university. Do you know who accredits universities? People inside the education industry. There is a stark difference between having a degree and being educated. The diploma attests to the fact that you paid for a degree and met the university requirements to obtain the degree. It says little about the value of your degree or whether you learned how to think. Becoming educated and informed is a lifelong journey. It's not a four-year program.

The institution from where you earned your degree, your field of study, and your performance may give the market clues to your success and ability in that program. It may also measure for the market a baseline to determine whether an employer should take a risk on you. Employers will rightly view one who goes to Harvard and studies business, graduating with high honors, in a kind light. The market might be less favorable to a graduate of Becker College with a degree in global citizenship.[3] Both institutions are private, "nonprofit" entities.

Going deep into debt for nearly any degree is a great risk, and it is a risk most young students don't appreciate. No responsible educator is opposed to people taking a gamble on themselves to obtain an education. No responsible educator or policy maker is opposed to responsible debt necessary for a student to procure the right education at the right price.

Americans must find the courage to oppose a culture that pushes kids into debt and churns out "degreed" citizens unable to think or find productive work to pay their debts. Indeed, that is the impetus for this book. Americans must take on an industry that has created this bureaucratic, self-serving "structural liberalism." We must inform the educational consumer while pushing the industry to reform. No single voice for reform will be strong enough, but "educated" consumers can drive the changes necessary.

There are innumerable books on student loan debt, and now there is a new, free-market industry out there to help consumers manage, consolidate, and reduce their debt service. Of course, for the next generation of college students, the key is to avoid this massive debt. Huge student loan debt ultimately delays car purchases, house purchases, consumer goods purchases, and the accrual of wealth.

Owning property is the primary method by which most people accrue wealth, and an appreciating home value often spurs more economic activity for both the homeowner and the overall economy. Student loan debt has not only the potential to strap an individual debtor, but it is likely to slow this economy, which is driven nearly 70 percent by consumer activity.[4]

The primary goal of every educational consumer must be to maximize value and reduce debt. Even today, in this horrific set of educational circumstances where an entire industry is saddling young people with debt to pay for a tenure class, many options are available for savvy students and families to obtain high-value skills at much lower costs. Here's the irony. If collective action were possible, smart consumers could reform this industry by simply making better, cheaper choices that force reform on the institutions.

Just 28 years ago, a 23-year-old going back to school for the first time had to begin, by necessity, at a community college. Economic and educational realities would force such a student into the community college system, a move that, ironically, would save such a student from debt, even if that person finished in law school, became an assistant law dean, ran a tech company, or became a legal expert on radio and TV. By the end of the 1990s that 23-year-old might have both a law degree and undergraduate degree for under $40,000. Remarkably, that is still possible today, for an educated consumer.

Most Americans who can and should go to college can and should get out of their undergraduate degree with less debt than a loan on a small, midsized, decently equipped car. A student loan payment should look more like a loan payment plan for owning a Toyota Corolla one might never drive, rather than a loan payment for a four-bedroom suburban house in which one will never live.

Part 2 of this book examines how to keep your debt low and how to obtain a high-value degree without wondering if you need to put off buying a house, car, or even getting married.

Chapter 11

What Is a Dubious Degree?

THE MARRIAGE OF STRUCTURAL
AND CULTURAL LIBERALISM

"As a white assistant professor of mostly white graduate students who will become higher education leaders, I work to dismantle whiteness in my curriculum, assignments and pedagogy," Linley explained, noting that in addition to her "white identity," she also draws on her "identities as a queer, able-bodied, cisgender woman" with a working-class background to construct her "teaching paradigm."[1] —academic insights of Iowa assistant professor Jodi Linley

Perhaps this book has misled you. It would be nearly impossible to have a book that discusses "structural liberalism" without some examination and examples of the more traditional, radical, "cultural" or "political" liberalism that has infected college campuses. Indeed, to appreciate the tenure tax, and the cost that "academic expression" has on our society we ought to hear from some of our college professors in the industry, "teaching" cutting-edge subjects to future debtors.

Professor Linley, who opens this chapter, is not even close to the worst example of political liberalism churning out dubious scholarship in a subject matter of limited value. Her utter drivel describing her educational philosophy is at best abuse of the English language and one of the finer collections of snobbery, idiocy, and irrelevancy ever cobbled together. Whatever her intellect, and no matter her expertise, she offers a university course for which there is no value—none. She ought not to have tenure in a 1960s cult.

What is a dubious degree? A dubious degree or field of study is one for which no one in the free market is hiring. Note, Professor Linley is producing graduate students to work in higher education. Of course she is. Higher education is nothing more than cultural leftists, teaching cultural leftism, and producing graduates whose only employment options are to be hired back into the system.

She isn't an outlier; she's what higher education produces when lifetime appointees choose like-minded comrades for other lifetime appointments. Make no mistake; the higher education industry is cranking out left-leaning radicals because it is hiring, retaining, and growing an army of "professors" in fields of study that are, again, of dubious market value.

While the focus of this book has been on the high financial cost of education caused by structural liberalism, we can't ignore the societal costs that political liberalism imposes within the higher education system of structural liberalism. Easy money, deep debt, underqualified students, and a bear market for social justice warriors is a certain recipe for an economic collapse of the student loan industry.

In the short term, riots, unrest, incivility, and protests are the immediate effects of an "everyone must go to college" culture. Why? We are cranking out degreed graduates for which there is no meaningful market of employment. Their primary skills include anger, distrust, and social radicalism that make them street warriors or professional agitators. The term social justice warrior, or SJW as we see it on the internet, has become a pejorative. To be clear, fighting against real injustice is the duty and obligation of the civil society, irrespective of one's political views.

Young students from ultra-liberal universities are no longer fighting injustice, they are finding injustice and intolerance in the views with which they disagree. This is what happens when we substitute critical thought for political liberalism and victimology as the focus of the American educational system.

While the primary interest of the education industry is to feed the lifestyle of the tenure and administrative class, its secondary focus is no more valuable to our society. The second mission of this industry is to advance a radical agenda of social warriors by creating, promoting, selling, and pushing a series of programs and degrees that have little market value. These programs teach students what to think rather than how to think, and they dump kids into a competitive, global job market with nothing but anger and debt.

What happens when adulthood is put off by unemployment, deep debt, and political hypertension? What happens when the promise of getting a college degree, no matter what, transforms into an equation of disappointment and joblessness over debt? What happens when we churn out global citizens, experts in gender studies, critical race theory, and dozens upon dozens of other "majors" into a job market that needs few, if any, of them? We are creating an army of social justice warriors, fueled by indoctrination.

Gone from many college campuses is a focus on critical thought. We used to teach kids how to think. Next, we moved to teaching them what to think. Now, on too many campuses and in too many majors, we are teaching them how to feel. What's worse, we are teaching them to reject "thinking" if it comes from an ideology with which they don't agree emotionally.

Americans simply do not think enough. In fact, in our politics, we feel, emote, and react, but we do very little thinking. This is a result of what is happening in our classrooms, manned by political liberals remaking our culture.

Even inside a top-tier law school where one sees some brilliant young minds at work, we see the decay of critical thought. Great minds can be impressive. However, it can be shocking when the cream of the crop all too often merely regurgitate a talking point devoid of analysis. Now, imagine what all the "non-cream of the croppers" are vomiting out. Too many numerically first-rate law students are ill-prepared to think critically and write objectively, using traditional methods of analysis. That reality reflects weak undergraduate programs.

Thinking is hard, and it requires introspection and analysis. It requires people to read, test a hypothesis, question conclusions, and ultimately find answers through drawing reasonable inferences from verifiable facts. As a country, we stink at this. In fact, we can hardly get the average political consumer to read past the title of a story, let alone dig into it and think about it. This is what our colleges are producing right now because too many people are in these dubious majors getting in touch with their feelings, checking their privilege, and learning to be compassionate.

The result of a country that does not and will not think is a decline in the quality of debate, the outcome of public policy, and the general civility that is essential to a free, prosperous people. Do we see evidence of this? Yes, every day our civility, decency, and debate draw closer to death.

The rise of political zealotry in a party-based system, rather than a thought-based system, is a key contributor to this decline of discourse. In a thought-based system, universities are the linchpin of producing students with the tools to think and analyze issues. When universities instead eschew classic, Western, liberal education and replace it with courses on the Kardashians, or other such tomfoolery, we get "degreed" non-thinkers.

Without independent thinking, we are reduced to political tribalism. Not only are Americans generally less thoughtful and therefore less informed, they are at many times less willing to be thoughtful and informed.

Never in human history has humanity had more tools of thought and analysis, or more information and facts at our fingertips, yet somehow, we are less informed. This reality is a derivative of a higher education system that myopically focuses on getting at feelings, rather than promoting independent reasoning. Indeed, one result that political liberals describe as "wealth inequality" is a direct result of structural and political liberalism and its mal-effect on driving thought.

In our system, we do have elite, world-class minds driving themselves toward advancements in every aspect of society. This is true in industry and academia. Don't be fooled; while structural liberalism is a bad deal for society as a whole, and higher education in particular, some students and thinkers are taking advantage of the information age to enhance their skills and accumulate more knowledge.

Put more simply, as the upper echelon continues to take advantage of the sum of human knowledge and technology, it leaves a greater and more pronounced gap between the knowledge havers and have-nots. In the mind of political liberals and a spoon-fed society, the answer to this achievement gap is to drive students to colleges, at any cost or for any subject, so that they too can compete in this global, innovative economy. That mindset wrongly assumes that all degrees and all higher education lead to the same result, and that no matter the cost, the debt is worth it. It is not.

Students obtaining business degrees from superior institutions are using new, innovative technologies and finding themselves working as interns and externs for institutions on the forefront of business, finance, and investing. These students often parlay those skills into jobs, and later into advanced degrees of value, like MBAs. They take these real skills and experiences out to a job market and use the sum of human knowledge and technology to maximize their personal opportunities within organizations that are working tirelessly to maximize corporate opportunities, profits, and innovation.

Those without market skills in a job market are falling further behind these innovative learners. And yes, those with no skills are falling even further behind. The phenomenon might best be explained thusly: the top crust of learners and thinkers, working in innovation, technology, and market-based skills, are pulling away from society at the same rapid pace that technology is pulling away. Yet those who are unskilled or semiskilled, are just as unskilled and semiskilled as 100 or 500 years ago.

The result of this reality is a gap of knowledge and market skills that continues to increase. A product of that gap, simply put, includes knowledge, skills, income, and obviously, wealth inequality. This is not to say other factors are not relevant to the issues and discussion on wealth distribution, but the unskilled laborer is much further behind today's innovators than they were just 20 years ago. Making this issue worse for the unskilled and semi-skilled is the reality that innovation itself is making jobs scarcer, while the pool of unskilled and semiskilled workers remains high.

These realities drive our cultural mandate that everyone get an education. Still getting a degree in something, at nearly any price, is not the right solution for society. It is rarely the right solution for individuals buried under debt, holding a degree of little value, and unable to find a market for skills not in demand. Structural liberalism is not creating an educated class, it is creating a debtor class. And the practical effect of that reality may be worse than we think.

While many young people are accruing deep debt to study subject matters of personal interest that are of little market value, they are forgoing skills and job opportunities in areas where the investment in the skill may be less, and the return may be higher. The loss of tradesmen, from electricians to plumbers and carpenters, or even oil riggers, reflects a diminished view our culture has for the value of the trades, even though the market value of those skills is often much higher than that degree in cisgender, LGBTQ studies on white male oppression. For sure, skills in the trades are cheaper to obtain and more market-ready.

Our structural liberalism, and a culture of "college at any cost," has Americans going to college at any cost because they are brainwashed by the industry that they must go to college. This alone is a dangerous proposition. Once there, colleges continue to create these "fields of study" that have no nexus between market demand and skills obtained. Instead of learning market-salable skills, students obtain debt, and in many cases they are filled with anger, entitlement, and an unhealthy cynicism of our capitalist structure and liberty-based, democratic republic.

Motivated by an ideology of big government entitlement, trained to see division on race, gender, orientation, religion, and class, these students are now "warriors." Unfortunately, they think their enemy is the people who have all the things they want. Instead of turning back to examine critically an industry that indebted them in these studies, they are on our streets rioting, fighting, protesting, chanting, and attacking everything they hate, resent, or distrust—without thought.

These social justice movements from BLM to Antifa are neither social nor do they know or understand basic concepts of justice. They are at war with thought and with the systems and structure that gave birth to liberty and our grand experiment to create and perfect it. When the student loan bubble bursts, and it will, this problem will get only worse.

Speaking of dubious majors and professors professing things of little or no value, behold this man formerly at the University of Tampa. He thought Texans deserved Hurricane Harvey for voting for Trump. Of course, in his hurry to get to Twitter (figure 11.1) and create a political splash, he failed to realize that most of metropolitan Houston wasn't really Trump country.

 **Ken Storey**
@klstorey

I dont believe in instant Karma but this kinda feels like it for Texas. Hopefully this will help them realize the GOP doesnt care about them

8/27/17, 2:32 PM from Winter Park, FL

2 Retweets **3** Likes

Figure 11.1.
Pic is screen capture. Can be found here too: https://twitter.com/TrotAlex/status/902258286975700993.

A visiting sociology professor who focuses on urban issues, "Professor" Storey was "relieved of his duties" by the university. That means he didn't have tenure with them.

Not surprisingly, those who collect the tenure tax and are not accountable for their lack of productivity find his dismissal "absolutely ridiculous." It's not. It's called the real world, and those with tenure ought to realize that with great power comes great responsibility.

Examples of left-leaning professors abound. When the ACLU tweeted out a cute picture of an innocent child waving a flag and holding a cute little doggy, suggesting, of course, that ACLU members see innocent children as our future, "Professor" Nyasha Junior typified the response of cultural liberalism we see too often from higher education. She met this harmless, well-intentioned tweet with a flippant response that can only be viewed as dangerous and ignorant, if not racist, to the extent those terms are not redundant.

Initial responses when people first saw her tweet drove some people to look her up in the hope that she wasn't really a professor. Unfortunately, a quick search showed she didn't merely work at Temple, she is a professor. Indeed, her tweet says so much with so little. However, for those who want a fuller

A White kid with a flag?!

Figure 11.2.
Source here: https://twitter.com/ACLU/status/900459882989600768.

understanding of her racialism, radicalism, and "work," they need only read her articles or look at her Twitter feed. It's easy to see what she professes. She is one of innumerable such cultural liberal warriors filling institutions with costs and shoveling hate and stupidity into kids who will quite literally pay for it for their entire lives. She's a racist who produces other racists.

Make no mistake about it; she undoubtedly doesn't think she is at all racist. She surely thinks she is combating racism. She likely thinks she is fighting racism, remarkably, by dividing by race, promoting racial division, and engaging in unuseful, race-based conduct. Her racial disdain and hate are what some have identified as "affirmative hate." That concept of affirmative hate is the cultural reality that members of formerly disadvantaged groups may engage in otherwise unacceptable conduct as some form of guilt-driven remediation. Sadly, we cannot move forward in unity on issues of race until we comprehensively address racism, both in its traditional form and in its new, hip, affirmative form. In so doing, we must no longer excuse or rationalize hate of any kind.

It's not just visiting professors and tenured professors, it is also tenured deans who run entire academic units who are part of the alt-left, higher education establishment. Meet the tenured dean of George Washington University's Elliott School of International Affairs. He thinks Trump is a white supremacist and Nazi sympathizer (figure 11.3).

The university's official Twitter page plugged his piece. To be clear, the institution of higher learning was #ElliottProud of the dean who called the president the "Nazi-in-Chief."

These are just recent examples of alt-leftism in the classroom. They are high profile because the hate, ignorance, radicalism, or intolerance they preach is usually confined to the classroom or shared among fellow radicals. Occasionally, however, these folks give us a peek into who the alt-left is and how its leaders really think. Yes, Dean Brigety, as you quoted Dr. Maya Angelou, "When someone shows you who they are, believe them!"[2]

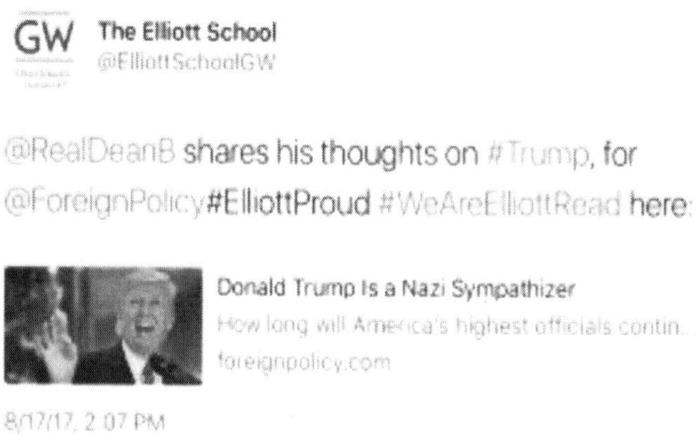

GW The Elliott School
@ElliottSchoolGW

 @RealDeanB shares his thoughts on #Trump, for
@ForeignPolicy #ElliottProud #WeAreElliottRead here:

 Donald Trump Is a Nazi Sympathizer
How long will America's highest officials contin...
foreignpolicy.com

8/17/17, 2 07 PM

Figure 11.3.
Source: https://twitter.com/ElliottSchoolGW/status/898265496625328128.

To combat racism and radicalism effectively, we must again become a society of thinkers. The education industry must make immediate reforms, and among those reforms must be a strong, comprehensive review of the programs, classes, courses, and majors that universities are pushing on our kids at great cost. We need tenure reform too, as the costs of these programs are reflected in a tenure tax where lifetime employment is the result of fields of study that universities create and feed, but never eliminate or reduce.

So-called "academic freedom" has a life estate at the intersection of radicalism and irresponsibility. You are paying the upkeep. As a result, America is getting more "educated," less informed, and deeper in debt. If you want to know why your tuition is so high, it's because stupid is expensive.

Cultural liberalism is the essential ingredient and the primary product of structural liberalism.

Part II

COMBATING THE HIGHER EDUCATION MONOPOLY: IS REFORM ENOUGH?

Chapter 12

Reform or Revolution?

THE COLONISTS TRIED REFORM. SOMETIMES, GREATNESS REQUIRES REVOLUTION.

He's a reformer.

Everyone calls for "reform" on issues of public policy. Americans think reform is a pleasant-sounding word that demonstrates our sophistication and ability to tinker on the edges of public policy and make improvements. Reform isn't a bad thing, and it is appropriate if we are discussing changing local school regulations related to how buses pick up and drop off students. Reform isn't valueless. America just has a very sparse history of successfully reforming a complete failure. When a structure or system of laws or government is so profoundly broken, reform is not the answer. Sometimes, you need a full revolution.

Americans are good at revolution.

Still, revolution scares modern Americans. It sounds angry, dangerous, violent, and a bit unpleasant in our urbane, sophisticated society. Revolution, however, doesn't have to be through force or by violent struggle. It can, but it doesn't have to mean that. As Americans, we did engineer the greatest revolution in world history, and yes, that one required some fighting. However, given our success at identifying structures that are a failure and burden in our culture, and burning them to the ground to fix and create a better system, we ought to embrace revolution over the weaker, less effective, and often unhelpful canard of reform.

In the 1990s, America had comprehensive immigration reform. Remember that? How did that reform work out? Congress did nothing to address the need to improve and streamline legal immigration. It did nothing to secure our borders. Congress did nothing to go after corporate abusers of immigrants or criminal networks that funnel immigrants into the country. Mostly, however, Congress did nothing but create more incentives for illegal immigrants to choose to break our laws and risk coming to America. In the end, the decision is easy for most living in desperation. The rewards far outweigh the risks.

In 1996, Congress passed an omnibus bill providing "comprehensive immigration reform." It reformed a failed system with reforms that failed to address the failure in the system. Immigration law needs a revolution, not reformation. The system has been irretrievably broken, and merely reforming it is like changing the oil and putting new tires on a car that was totaled in an accident and lost in a flood. They did something, they just didn't accomplish anything.

More than 20 years later, the country is again fighting and jousting over immigration reform from walls, to DACA, to E-Verify, to visa lotteries, to chain migration and beyond. No one yet is talking about burning the system to the ground and starting from scratch by identifying how America would build a strong, sustainable, commonsense set of immigration policies that meet the needs of Americans. They are stuck on the idea of "comprehensive reform."

A higher education revolution must not get likewise bogged down in an academic exercise about reforms on the margins. The industry does a terrible job of creating useful academic programs, at an affordable price, that attract and retain the right students and teach them skills useful in a job market. If we want to do that, we need revolution rather than reform. We need to start over, not merely start discussing how to tinker on the edges of a broken system that puts our global competitiveness at risk while indebting our population.

America must dream big. We must see the big picture and understand that our great educational landscape doesn't need to be touched up. We need a whole new canvas, and we must start with broad strokes and bright new colors. Mostly, we need a new, innovative design. Likewise, that design must be nimble enough to change as needed now, and in the future, as markets require. An education revolution must start now, but it must also be an ongoing endeavor. America must constantly work to create for individual students of merit a system where they can obtain the skills they need to compete in global markets.

Revolution is hard.

Most people are not drawn to revolution until desperation forces them there. Revolution comes when the misery index in any situation reaches an unbearable limit even for a strong, determined segment of society. It may be that we are not yet ready for an education revolution because the debt crisis has not yet exploded on our most recent graduates.

As early as 2003, for example, Republicans took to the floor of the House and insisted that Freddie Mac and Fannie Mae needed reform. They warned of destabilization in the housing market and the possibility of structural failure if Congress didn't step in with new regulations and safeguards. Imagine that, the Republicans looking for more regulation. This was all because the culture of a homeownership society created both an expectation and entitlement to owning a home, even if you are a bad bet and have no means to pay the loans.

No one listened.

By 2005 real estate markets began to fall, and by 2007 they had tanked nearly everywhere. By the summer of 2008, the great recession was on, and it was tied ever so closely to a cultural myth and expectation that every American can and should own a home. Books and movies have been made about all the various causes of the collapse, but it began with the structural liberalism of the "homeownership society." Now, we have a crippling student loan debt problem, and yet we keep raising prices and going deeper in debt. The bubble will burst, and we can wait to react or we can take on this problem in higher education.

It is time to plan, and it is time to work toward that revolution so we may reap the rewards as a society and provide a softer landing for those hurt by the indebtedness. The great thing about the plan in this book is that the individual consumer can create his or her own revolution right now.

Students and parents can use smart strategies to obtain great skills at a reasonable price while we work on the revolution. Moreover, in the instance of higher education, we can make some easy "reforms" on the margins that will help institutions and consumers in the short run, before a full-scale revolution may be necessary or even possible.

Part 2 of this book looks at strategies for individual students and families to grab from the revenue predators' skills that will serve students and do so at prices that make sense. At the same time, the book proposes global changes, some revolutionary in nature, and some merely reformist in nature. Some embrace deregulation, and others require regulation. One goal is to change the functional operation of institutions of higher education. These proposals are aimed at the industry, its accreditors, and those in the best position to incentivize change.

In the end, the primary focus of our educational revolution must be to place the interests of the educational consumer above all other stakeholders.

Chapter 13

Why Are Deregulation and Reregulation Essential in Higher Education?

Just because you don't get a bill marked "regulation tax" doesn't mean you don't pay one.

REGULATION: THE HIDDEN TAX ON EDUCATION

The Federal Acquisition Rules, known to lawyers and federal contractors as the "FAR," are an awesome collection of the rules your government sets out that govern how a company or individual may contract with it and compete against others who seek to contract with it. The government spends about $4 trillion a year, and much of that is purchased through contracts with corporations and entities looking to sell their goods for a profit. To do that, a business must understand the FAR, comply with it, and be prepared to absorb the costs of compliance with it. Not surprisingly, all the costs of compliance with FAR regulations are baked into the bids for goods and services and then passed along to the taxpayer.

Regulations are a tax on productivity. They create costs that businesses must absorb. Now, you are thinking, well, millions of businesses do that, don't they? Yes, indeed they do. Businesses, contrary to the thinking of progressives, don't pay taxes. You do. In education, the "costs" of regulation are ultimately borne by the educational consumer.

In a quick but necessary lesson on economics, a business has few options when its costs go up. It can try to reduce its own costs, or it can raise prices. Some progressives think businesses just absorb the additional cost of taxes and regulation by reducing profits. They do not. Businesses exist to profit if they can. Indeed, businesses have a fiduciary duty to their owners to make sound business decisions that will lead to profitability.

Faced with increased costs, businesses may be forced to reduce profits or salaries. Of course, most businesses don't profit like the left thinks, and reducing profitability isn't a great option. Even if a company profits, reducing those profits is not a great choice if the company has shareholders to whom it must account, or lenders, or private equity offerings looking to lend, purchase, or invest on terms based on profits.

When government imposes costs on business, a company is primarily left with two choices. Stuck with a new cost, be it a tax, regulation, or rise in the cost of its suppliers' goods and services, a company can raise prices of its goods and services, or it can cut costs. When a company faces new, higher costs, it will often look to squeeze out its own costs. We see this in job cuts, reduction of benefits, stalled expansion, automation, or reducing growth and jobs. That's the real world.

As we have discussed in this book, higher education doesn't reduce costs. It doesn't live in the real world because the tenure tax is one it can't reduce. Sometimes, on the margins, a university might cut a secretary, hold back raises, or put off construction of new academic buildings and programs, but mostly, it just keeps raising prices. Why? Well, its competitors keep raising prices too, and the federal government keeps giving its customers low-interest loans to pay the bills. Moreover, as we discussed, the biggest cost is in tenured faculty, and institutions can't cut them.

One easy way to reduce costs in public education is to deregulate it in part. Higher education is a highly regulated industry where the Department of Education, through accrediting entities, creates rules, benchmarks, and requirements that drive up costs like mad on institutions. Of course, the purported trade-off on any regulation is that the benefit of a given regulation offsets the burden or cost. Indeed, that might be true for a few regulations, but as a collection, regulations do not. Returning to the law school example, we can illustrate how regulation drives up costs and thus becomes a tax on the educational consumer.

The American Bar Association (ABA) accredits law schools. In fact, every seven years, every accredited law school in the country must undergo a reaccreditation process by the ABA.[1] The process of reaccreditation is not fun. It is costly, time-consuming, and can result in thousands of man-hours for compliance, which sometimes takes years to finally obtain. Law School reaccreditation finishes with a site visit by an accreditation team who ultimately spends 2 or 3 days at the institution doing the best it can to understand everything there is to know about your program.

The ABA team looks at its findings from this comprehensive process and compares those findings to the lengthy, ever-changing ABA rules and standards that the ABA promulgates. Of course, the every-seven-year visit is grueling, but it is made more grueling by the institution having to produce proof of its compliance with hundreds of standards the ABA designs to ensure that an accredited law school meets a minimum standard of excellence to keep its accreditation.

Once the team finishes the site visit, within a reasonable period, it writes a full report. In that report it notes any issues or deficiencies. If significant issues arise, a school may be forced to make program changes or hires. It may be forced to spend money too. If the school administration and the site team disagree about the application of the standards or a school's success in meeting them, the ABA and the school may exchange letters and additional information until such time as the ABA agrees a school is in compliance. That assumes the ABA and the institution ever agree that compliance is met. If it is not, then the school must agree to remediation and changes in order to ensure it complies with the regulations and keeps its accreditation.

Harvard, Yale, and Stanford too must go through this process, which on its face is a complete waste of time for these institutions. This is not to suggest that any institution should be exempt from rules or standards if all are not. However, the notion that three of our most recognized institutions might no longer be accredited is an absurdity.

The ABA accreditation process sends its site team to a school and that team drills down on a host of subjects, including those that quite literally have nothing to do, in any way, with the quality of the education. Many of the rules are either political dogma or worse, protectionism, designed to insulate the tenure class, without regard to costs or performance. Obviously, examples are necessary to demonstrate this provocative point.

In Mason Law's most recent ABA evaluation, the initial site-team report noted that Mason had not done enough to demonstrate it was actively recruiting female faculty members, either in its full-time faculty or in its adjunct faculty. Ultimately, the assertion was proven incorrect. In fact, the gender diversity of Mason's Law faculty is completely on par with its competitors.

Likewise, Mason worked very hard in the industry to find, identify, and attract female scholars who work in the law and economic field. Even if Mason had not done so, why would it matter for the quality of the law program what Mason does to attract female faculty members?

One might argue that if Mason were actively discriminating against female applicants, that might matter. However, the ABA seemed to be obsessed with the issue, and it was hell-bent on making the institution prove it did all it could to attract people based on their gender, which is the essence of the political liberalism that undergirds structural liberalism.

On the protectionism front, the ABA has standards related to "security of position" for many positions. Moreover, it has a requirement that first-year law courses, which in law school are generally the same subjects nationally, be taught by regular tenured faculty. That is, a law school can't merely hire the greatest contract faculty member or adjunct on earth, it must use a tenured faculty member to teach these courses. The cost of forcing schools to use tenured professors to do the job a nontenured instructor can perform is astronomical.

The obvious theory behind the ABA mandate on "tenured faculty" is the idea that tenured faculty are superior, and most importantly, enjoy greater academic freedom. Certainly, no one enjoys greater academic freedom than tenured faculty. However, if one wanted to open a law school in Virginia on a metro line, and he or she was able to get 25 of the best lawyers in the DC area to work as adjuncts, why would the ABA care about whom such an innovator hires? Shouldn't the ABA be evaluating the quality of the instruction and not the terms of the contract with the instructor?

The DC metropolitan area is crawling with some of the best legal minds in America. As such, DC-based law schools enjoy an endless supply of world-class lawyers who work as adjuncts or term faculty. This includes federal judges, law firm managing partners, and subject matter experts in nearly every legal field. On any given night at George Mason Law School, the building is teeming with outstanding, real, accomplished, impressive lawyers teaching students as adjuncts.

Mason's night program is ranked in the top five in the country because of this outstanding advantage it has in its legal market. So many great lawyers want to teach, without giving up their rewarding careers. Nearly every one of them, whether they know it or not, would never be considered for a tenured faculty position, where writing a particular type of legal scholarship is still, remarkably, the primary criterion for full-time, tenured law professors. These legal experts hired as adjuncts are a dramatically cheaper option for instruction, and in most cases, are actually better instructors.

From 1996 until the middle of 2016, demand by students to take adjunct classes was always strong. In fact, like it or not, the classes taught by adjuncts are often more popular among students. Tenured faculty would explain this phenomenon by telling you that some adjuncts were easier graders and less demanding. However, students have an unquenchable thirst to learn from, work with, and connect to practitioners. One cannot fool the market. In a deregulated environment, or an environment where only quality matters, a law school like Mason could take advantage of these much cheaper teaching options for more of its classes.

Why doesn't higher education allow universities to do this? Look at the economics of this opportunity. Mason used to pay its adjuncts roughly $1,260 a credit. Thus, most adjuncts made a little under $3,800 to teach a three-credit class. A tenured law professor making $150,000 in salary commands nearly $203,000 in total compensation. Moreover, such a professor is paid on a nine-month basis, and he or she receives additional research money in the summer.

At Mason, a tenured law professor must teach only nine credits in an academic year (not a semester). In some cases, professors obtain "teaching relief" if they take part in other duties in aid of the administration of the school or for special projects.

Working solely off the example of total compensation above, a tenure-class professor making $150,000 a year costs Mason over $22,000 a credit, or about $67,000 per class. That's a staggering $63,000 more per three-credit class than it might cost Mason to staff that class with a leading legal eagle from DC's teeming legal market.

Is it possible that a law student receives over $63,000 more in teaching value from the tenured professor? It is possible,but it's highly unlikely. Is it possible that the law student has a giant tuition bill because of the cost of the tenured faculty member versus the cost of a comparable adjunct? It's a 100 percent certainty.

This comparison will bring howls of objection from the tenure class. To be sure, a tenured professor often, if not always, makes other contributions to the school. He or she might help forge curriculum, look at academic standards, advise students, write articles, and help to increase the reputational value of the institution. Thus, a straight comparison of cost per class against an adjunct who only teaches that class may not be apples to apples. But in reality, none of those other contributions can change the value equation to tilt or tip in the favor of the tenure system.

The ABA foists this system on schools to protect students and ensure quality, purportedly. Just who is the ABA to tell Mason, or anyone, who is best for the teaching job? To the extent accrediting agencies are there to give approval to the quality of a program, that's fine. When they dictate how a program must be taught, by whom, and at what cost, that is when regulation tips from protecting to protectionism. Forcing law schools to create a system that protects the tenure class merely drives up debt.

These ABA regulations are a product of protectionism and political liberalism. It's a vicious circle. These ABA regulations and panels come from the industry, and they serve the industry. Together they are components of structural liberalism.

No responsible administrator, even a conservative, would insist that higher education go unchecked. Indeed, if this book makes any case, it is that the industry is self-serving. *It requires responsible regulation and oversight.* The necessary changes might best be described not merely as deregulation, but as reregulation. Some forms of regulation are essential, just like some forms of government are essential. We need regulations to protect consumers from these entities.

Even in a free market, it is obvious that higher education entities have a superior advantage in dealing with customers who don't have every possible tool in the market to evaluate the true quality or value of an institution on their own. A vigilant consumer can learn more than ever before about institutions, and the need for oversight as it relates to quality is not nearly as strong as it might once have been. The biggest regulatory need in higher education is to protect students from predatory lending and debt. The greatest deregulatory need is to return control of the institution to management.

Before turning away from examples that support deregulation and moving toward suggestions on how to improve the delivery of educational services, another example of the failure and cost of ABA oversight is essential.

CULTURAL LIBERALISM VERSUS STRUCTURAL LIBERALISM

Cultural liberalism is an integral part of the much larger structural liberalism that the book examines. However, just because cultural liberalism is a part or subset of structural liberalism does not mean the two cannot, at times, be at odds. That is to say, sometimes the structural liberalism components of regulation, protectionism, paternalism, and consumer protection can become adverse to the cultural or political liberalism that undergirds and is the foundation of structural liberalism.

Structural liberalism and cultural liberalism sit at a dangerous intersection with the ABA. The ABA creates rules and standards under both headers. Sometimes, those rules and standards can be at odds with each other. When rules implicating structural liberalism collide with rules implicating cultural liberalism, it is not hard to predict which standard trumps the other at the ABA. Not surprisingly, the critical purpose of ensuring quality and protecting consumers falls behind the political agenda often advanced by cultural liberalism.

In the early 2000s, the ABA conducted a site visit of Mason Law. It came away concluding that Mason was not doing enough to attract diversity in its admissions. It found that Mason did not have sufficient numbers of African Americans enrolled in its JD classes. Mind you, cultural liberals actually believe that such numbers exist. That is to say, cultural liberalism teaches and subscribes to the belief that when a given class or identity of people are underrepresented in a given pool, that some form of systematic discrimination is, by itself, the answer.

The ABA further suggested Mason Law was not doing enough to improve what the ABA thought was Mason's poor performance in both recruiting and successfully landing minority applicants. Make no mistake, George Mason, a law school with a "conservative" bent, then sitting in the second tier, did not have a large number or percentage of black or Hispanic students.

It is constitutionally questionable, and educationally incorrect, to assume that Mason, or any institution, has an obligation to actively pursue any group based on race, color, or gender. Putting that larger debate to the side, the book focuses on how the ABA attempted to address the issue, and why the ABA's method was ill-informed, devoid of substantive analysis, and the result of cultural liberalism that permeates the regulatory body.

Mason Law, at the time, agreed to make a greater effort at recruitment. Indeed, it did that. In doing so, it spent a great deal of money chasing unicorns. However, before being forced to spend that money, Mason properly made its record to the ABA. It explained that it had very little success in these areas with the ABA's defined identity groups for innumerable reasons, none of which resulted from bias or a lack of effort. Indeed, among the most obvious reasons were a lack of interest in the school's program and its political reputation. Of course, other reasons played a more obvious role that the ABA simply did not want to consider.

Mason Law rightfully pointed out that high-quality minority applicants with whom it spoke and who also met the school's academic standards were nearly impossible to recruit because these candidates were receiving generous scholarship offers from much higher-ranked, better-known institutions. At those schools, the institutions were both willing and able to absorb lower academic numbers to increase minority enrollment. They could do so because those schools could maintain their relative rank by admitting even more, higher-credentialed candidates. Mason, like many other second-tier and smaller law schools could not—and still cannot do that.

To understand this intricate relationship of rank and student quality, one needs to recognize that law school rankings, particularly those done by *US News*, command enormous market value. Whatever law administrators think of the *US News* rankings, those rankings are gospel to the consumer. Moreover, the consumer thinks the law school ranked 38 is significantly better than school 52 or 45. When a school's rank jumps, the school often foolishly plays into this misperception by marketing that rank. This moment of pride and marketing opportunity only serves to cement as gospel a ranking system that is deeply, profoundly, unapologetically baseless.[2]

In the very early 2000s, Mason was in the second 50 law schools among ranks, and it commanded very little national attention based on quality. It worked hard to raise its academic standards because the academic quality of the student body an institution admits represents a large chunk of the rank score, though that chunk of the score is not as large as the deeply flawed system of ranking the academic reputation of an institution through a survey to and among competitors and judges.

For a school like Mason, a minority applicant with a 3.4 GPA and a 159 to 160 LSAT was a great student. Indeed, any student with those numbers was an ideal target at that time. Ironically, Mason looked at the qualifications of a student and not his or her color. Still, a minority applicant with those numbers in the early 2000s was going to a top-20 law school. Not only could the student choose among nationally known and ranked schools, he or she was going to get major financial aid to attend such an institution.

Mason didn't have much money, and at that time it gave very few scholarships. It was and is a small state school. It likewise had a negligible endowment, and a small active alumni base from which to draw. For schools like Mason, they were forced to fight for minority students with bigger institutions. The fight was a mismatch.

Minority applicants could either choose the second-tier Mason and receive little money, or an applicant could go to a huge brand-name school. Indeed, many of these bigger brands filled their own minority mandates by leveraging their market power and endless supply of overqualified students to level off the class academic credentials. For example, while those impressive academic numbers might have been perfect for admission to Mason Law, had the student accepted, those numbers were below the admission criteria of top 20 law schools.

The top-20 schools simply admitted the lesser-qualified students and then found higher-ranked students to level off to their preferred *average GPA and LSAT scores*. Lesser-ranked, poorer schools with much smaller applicant pools didn't have that luxury.

George Mason literally had nothing they could offer such students. No reasonable student, of any demographic, would turn down a scholarship from a much higher-ranked school just to attend Mason. Since the applicant pool was very shallow among certain demographics, Mason was left with few minority students to attract, unless Mason dramatically lowered its admissions criteria for students much lower in the pool.

Besides the obvious Constitutional and ethical problems with admitting academically unqualified students based solely on race, doing so would have punished Mason in the ranks because Mason, as a small second-tier law school, did not have an endless supply of law students with much higher GPAs and LSATs to offset the lower-credentialed students. In this scenario, one need not be a former law dean or an ABA accreditor to figure, then, why Mason couldn't draw in larger numbers of minority students.

Indeed, the reason why Mason had lower minority student enrollment was minorities had far better options, and they wisely took those options.

Likewise, Mason was not capable of dropping its standards to get deeper into the minority pool without compromising its rank. It simply could not accept students dramatically outside its academic standards just to inflate minority numbers to reach an ABA ideal quota based on social engineering born of irresponsible cultural liberalism. This should have been obvious to the ABA. It didn't care.

Still, the ABA demanded that schools work to attract minority candidates and it has a standard requiring schools to do so. It also has, and at that time had, a standard that prevents law schools from admitting students to their programs if the institutions know the student cannot compete in the program based on an applicant's proven academic credentials.

When Mason reminded the ABA of its own academic standard designed to protect students from having schools take their money and fail them out, what do you think the ABA did to resolve this obvious conflict?

Faced with a conflict in its rules between advancing a political agenda or protecting students, the ABA went all in on the cultural liberalism. It insisted Mason must do more to recruit minority applicants, irrespective of their projected ability to succeed. In short, the ABA essentially forced Mason to take people with academic numbers that it knew presented a higher rate of failure. In so doing, of course, the ABA also knew that Mason would have to spend even more resources to help support those students. It makes one wonder, who accredits the accreditors?

Mason Law was faced with a choice when confronted by the ABA's cultural command that collided with its consumer protection regulation: have a public fight over its "minority" enrollment and suffer the false accusation that a "conservative" law school wouldn't admit minorities or acquiesce to the ABA demand and choose the ABA's political agenda over its consumer protection standard.

Mason knew, as any sentient accreditor also would know, that Mason admitted students with very strong academic numbers and that the law school had very difficult grading standards. Any student, irrespective of color, who fell well outside those admission numbers would struggle, and Mason had ample data to support that fact. In short, what Mason said was, you are asking us to break your own rule to protect students who cannot compete academically to meet another rule you have that mandates a socially liberal outcome.

Faced with the Hobsonian choice, Mason expanded the pool of admits. It was not a success. It was not a success because Mason was right. Students who perform far outside the proven academic ranges of successful students cannot be expected to succeed just because an institution or group of social engineers want them to. The ABA, as you can see, like many academic accrediting agencies, have rules that reflect the cultural liberalism of an industry in charge of its own compliance.

Just as we should not let friends hire friends, we should not let an industry infected with structural and cultural liberalism regulate itself, creating a series of rules and standards that do little to protect consumers, but do much to drive social agenda and, ironically, create costs and failure in the system.

A BLUEPRINT FOR BETTER REGULATION
IN HIGHER EDUCATION

1. On accreditation, eliminate rules, guidelines, and standards that do not reflect solely on academic and institutional performance.
2. Deregulate all requirements related to tenure or security of position. Permit institutions to make those individual decisions. Institutions can offer tenure as they see fit, or they can hire and increase adjunct and term professors.
3. Get the government out of the student loan business or reopen competition.
4. Increase regulation on private entities offering student loans with an eye toward stopping predatory lending.
5. Require institutions to publish teaching loads and develop a uniform standard to reflect investment of institutions on teaching and instruction.
6. Require institutions to give mandatory counseling on all student loans, to require disclosure of job data, market data, salary data, and debt ratios of prospective majors.
7. Require institutions to provide to students a comparative analysis of the cost of their major with any state institution, including 2- and 4-year degrees, from which state the student is applying.
8. Eliminate any federal money from any institution that offers in-state tuition to illegal immigrants and require that any federal grant be moved from any institution that does not comply.
9. Create a Presidential Commission on Higher Education to look at accreditation reform in order to refocus reform on academic excellence and reducing costs, while also refocusing accreditation on academic standards rather than social outcomes.

Chapter 14

Do We Really Need Student Loan Reform?

Not all majors are created equal.[1]

Giving eighteen-year-old kids subsidized student loans to study any-thing, anywhere, at any cost is a practice that must end today. All education is not created equal. All institutions and majors are not of the same value (figure 14.1), and not every student is a good risk for college. That is particu-larly true when we match the strength of a student to the weakness of certain majors at certain institutions.

Read this correctly, because it is the exact opposite of the cultural obses-sion in which we live where Americans are pushing kids into any college to study anything.

IT. MUST. STOP.

It should be harder, not easier, to get a college student loan. The burden is on the buyer to show both his or her worthiness for the risk, and that the risk and value of the investment are worth the loan terms. Likewise, since institutions are immediate recipients of the loans, institutions should be required to prove the value and worth of the investment, on a major-by-major basis. In fact, these loans make educational institutions third-party benefi-ciaries. As such, they should have obligations to prove the value of the invest-ment to diminish the risk.

If America is going to subsidize student loans, then Americans need a much better system to ensure value for the investment and to help make sure that our willingness to subsidize debt is responsible. We need a system that does not push unsuspecting and unqualified students into huge debt that makes no sense for a degree of little value, from institutions of a dubious reputation. We must make most loans harder to obtain for weak schools and underperforming majors. We must tie the loans and rates to the risk and outcome. This would be a student loan revolution.

Majors With The Highest Earnings

Majors With The Lowest Earnings

Figure 14.1.   Not all majors are created equal.[42]
Source: http://www.npr.org/sections/money/2013/09/10/219372252/the-most-and-least-lucrative-college-majors-in-1-graph.

It would reduce the number of student loans, or it would increase the cost of the loans if the risk is unpalatable. Risky loans would not get a subsidy, forcing students into a private market where risk becomes, as it should, costlier and unsubsidized. Moreover, institutions that cannot prove the value of the major would lose students and be forced to resize or eliminate certain majors. Student loan standards can be established to give guidelines that will prevent students from investing unwisely or at too high a cost.

Cutting off the unchecked federal influx of cheap dollars will have an instant effect on efficiency. It will force institutions to make significant changes. Right now, institutions can keep building programs and adding costs because they are subsidized through predatory, unchecked lending that allows students to keep paying an institution's bills while the student accrues crushing debt. Yes, this may mean that some students won't go where they want to study what they want. That might be a good thing. Or it may mean that marginally qualified students who want to take a risk on a suspect major will have to borrow more and learn of the steep risk in such borrowing before being permitted to accrue debt.

The critical component of cutting off and reducing federal loans to suspect institutions, or for dubious majors, is that the institutions must face down a system of permanent employees and suspect majors with an eye toward reform, if not revolution. Some will embrace that option, others will not. Some institutions have no such need for reform or revolution. At the top of our academic food chain, nothing will change the institutions with multi-billion-dollar endowments and international reputations. However, lesser-known institutions will have to find ways to cut costs and tailor programs that meet the needs of students and industry.

One simple reform in this system is to increase dramatically the subsidies we give for student loans to students who attend trade schools and community colleges. If you want more of something, subsidize it. Let's encourage bad bets to move into the less costly, lower-risk institutions and programs.

On the one hand, when subsidies and loans are reduced to weaker four-year institutions with unproven majors, money will be available to drive more students to community college where costs are lower, and where the cost of failure or choosing and changing a major won't lead to lifetime debt. Obviously, this sea change in lending will cause an increase in costs at these institutions, but the relative value is well worth the change in the incentive structure.

In addition, this new competition from two-year colleges and vocational schools will force state institutions and small private colleges to refocus their programs and to find ways to both cut costs and be more competitive in offering students majors that matter at a value that is sensible.

None of this change will be easy. As we know, institutions thriving in the current system have market power and entrenched constituencies who will fight change. They have massive numbers of lifetime employees who can't easily be cut or in some cases can't be cut at all. This reallocation of federal financing, hopefully, will drive the next subject of this book, which is tenure reform.

My reforms for the student loan industry are based on making it harder to get riskier loans, a practice we should embrace. They keep government-subsidized loans, but they refocus those loans toward value majors and value institutions, choking off the free ride and free cash to other institutions. Likewise, we need to open robust private loan competition to give students more options, including allowing students hell-bent to take a huge risk on themselves to do so, in that circumstance, taking the risk for themselves.

Subsidized or not, no student loan should be dispersed without counseling on debt and the effects of such debt. That counseling would require that students sign off and understand the current market value of their proposed majors and fields of study.

Chapter 15

Can We Really Reform Tenure?

Tenure reform is the holy grail of higher education reform. If you want to reduce costs but still maintain excellence in higher education, you must have a smart, strong, well-compensated, protected, productive, and innovative class of professors who are accountable for performance and subject to market forces.

Tenure does not provide the same value to the institutions or the debtors who fund it that the tenure class receives in return. That's simply the truth. As we discussed earlier, all the benefits of tenure inure to those who have it and all the burdens are borne by the institutions that give it. In too many cases, the lifetime job and protection of the tenure class is not a successful bargain for the institution or the educational consumer.

With tenure, only the professor is permitted to get out of the deal. If an institution gets a dud, it's stuck with the dud. If the institution gets a rock star, and there are many, the institution could lose that professor at any time. Such a deal makes no sense for institutions or consumers. They exist because the industry puts itself and its members ahead of the students, the tuition payer, and the taxpayer.

Before setting out on two paths to take on tenure, one that is more about reform and one that is all about revolution, we must look at why tenure reform is so difficult. First, tenure does provide the best shield for protecting academic freedom. A tenured law professor is a nearly bulletproof law professor. His scholarship and academic freedom permit him to do and say nearly anything, and it is mostly impossible, as we discussed, to punish him for it.

THE CASE FOR TENURE?

In working as a nontenured, administrative law dean, by pure happenstance an assistant dean found himself embroiled in controversy with a powerful public figure.[1] This came about because of the dean's role of providing legal and political commentary on radio, TV, and print. The facts surrounding these events provide evidence for the call for protecting academic freedom, and they support, seemingly, a bright-line rule like the tenure system.

The sitting attorney general (AG) of Virginia called the university president pressuring the president to punish or fire the dean because of his legal analysis and political opinion in an op-ed written about the attorney general's action to aid and support in-state tuition for illegal aliens. Had the dean been a "tenured" law professor, the president would have been obliged to tell the AG to go pound sand. Indeed, the president should have done that. However, he didn't have to defend that assistant dean, and he didn't have to like or accept an opinion of a person with whom he strongly disagreed, because that assistant dean was not tenured.

The institution where the assistant dean worked was also where he had graduated from years before. He was the elected graduation speaker chosen by his law class as a student. He went on to clerk, work at a large international law firm, and even become president of the law alumni association. That same dean helped Mason form its now most successful, student-oriented law center aimed at protecting intellectual property. By 2014, he had also been elected the "faculty" speaker by the graduating class given his teaching performance in the classroom.

None of that changed his status, which was that of an at-will employee. He was never a tenured employee or on the tenure track. He never asked to be, nor would he have been considered for such a position in the current hiring system, as he was not a published scholar in the field of law and economics. Through a bit of luck, the dean wound up helping the local NPR affiliate on analyzing the trial of former Virginia governor Bob McDonnell. That six-week stint as a legal analyst resulted in innumerable radio and TV appearances on numerous subjects.

The dean was happy to do it, and the university wildly publicized his many appearances. At one point, the public relations department told the dean he had a quote about the case carried in over 100 publications by the AP (Associated Press). He was doing local radio and TV, and he even had appearances on Fox Business News with Charles Payne and with Neil Cavuto. Again, the university heralded those appearances, and those appearances are still linked to its webpages. How good was the dean at this role? The university also began paying a PR company that would work to get him even more appearances in print, on radio, and on TV. The university paid a lot for that.

Still, many of the dean's appearances were organic. That is, media outlets sought him out for comment and contribution without working through the PR company.

In February of 2015, he wrote an op-ed taking the Virginia legislature to task for permitting the attorney general to draft an advisory opinion that could have the full force of law, resulting in changing Virginia's domiciliary statute. The change in interpretation by the AG would permit illegal aliens living in the Commonwealth to claim domiciliary status, and thus be eligible for in-state tuition as foreign nationals living in the state illegally.

The AG complained to the university president, who called the law school dean in on the carpet. The university then shut down the assistant dean's appearances. It prevented him from appearing on radio, TV, or in print using the Mason name. That, however, did not stop news networks from calling him or from him appearing. By January of 2016, the new dean decided to eliminate the assistant dean's position after changing his title, limiting his contact with students, and giving him party-planning activities failed to get him to quit.

If you want to know what tenure exists for, it exists to stop that type of retaliation and punishment on a whim by administrators who may fire a person for any bad reason, including the abuse of power by a state-elected official applying political pressure to a state university president. The entire sorry event reflects poorly on the AG, the president, and both the old and new law school deans. It was an embarrassment. However, the reality is that nearly all nontenured employees are subject to these whims, for better or worse. And while Mason handled this terribly, one might say that a president and a dean who no longer think an employee valuable ought to have the right to let him go.

One tenured professor said at the time, "What would they do if I took the same piece, published it, and put my name on it?" The answer was simple. The university would not have done a thing. That's why tenure protects academics from the arbitrary reactions of administrators who might shut down discussion on uncomfortable topics or research. Assuring that administrators can't do that is essential to promoting academic views and opinions with which some do not agree.

That protection of academic freedom is something an administrative, nontenured dean did not have, but something that would have prevented his dismissal. Still, Mason Law is surviving without him, and will continue to do so. It is true that most competent institutions might have promoted such a dean or fought to keep such an asset. Mason didn't. The lesson, however, is not that bad actors sometimes take bad actions, it is that no assistant dean is irreplaceable, and neither is any professor, dean, president, or attorney general.

You will rarely, if ever, meet a person who really is irreplaceable at any job. Likewise, you will rarely, if ever, meet a person or professor who should keep his or her job forever, irrespective of value.

On one hand, the assistant dean's story might be an argument for tenure protections. On the other hand, it is proof that these lifetime protections serve only to stifle innovation and change for unnecessary protections. Why are they unnecessary? Because no one is irreplaceable, and thus the cost of non-replaceability is always too high. Yes, without tenure, weak presidents and self-serving, small-minded deans will sometimes cut loose an administrator, academic, or young scholar who doesn't deserve it.

Academic leadership already suffers from the horrific reality that university presidents and deans are often promoted to their position based on years of being academics, even if they have no administrative, business, or leadership skills. Friends hire friends. And the result is a costly, inefficient system.

Academic positions where tenure does not exist show that an institution can replace people, make mistakes, and replace them again—just as one might in business. The only difference between this example and business, is that smart businesses hire to ensure performance and profit, and not merely for friendship and ideology.

A system where professors are accountable is a system that will undoubtedly result in some unfair, stupid terminations. That happens in the real world. Sometimes business gets hiring and firing dead wrong. Sometimes it lets people go without understanding their full value, and other times business makes decisions that are costly, rather than profitable. If business can work on that model, so too can academia.

With a tenure system, once an institution grants tenure, it eats that decision for life, at an incredible cost, and with no assurance that the minimum productivity it hoped to receive from the scholar will take place.

There is not a single law professor, among many outstanding professors at George Mason or any other school, whom a law school could not fire today and still survive. Some would be true losses. Here's a secret, however: you will rarely find a single law student, as a student or as an alumnus, who attended a school just to study with professor X. Yes, a faculty's reputation might be a factor in school selection, or an individual faculty member's reputation might influence a student to take a particular class, but the market for law students is not driven by individual professors, and neither is the overwhelming majority of the higher education market.

Among the many great scholars in law, nearly none are attracting large swaths of students who will only attend a certain law school to study with a certain professor. That is likewise true in many fields. Now, it is true that in certain discrete fields, and in certain world-class research institutions and graduate programs, the elite of the elite work hard to study with or under the world's most renowned professors. The slice of students in that pool is remarkably small, and the slice of professors who meet that description is even smaller.

THE MARKET IS THE BEST PROTECTION OF VALUE

No one came to study law at George Mason because of Dean Polsby or Dean Henry Butler. Likewise, they didn't go there to study with Assistant Dean Richard Kelsey. And here is the truth: there is a critical market protection for scholars whose names are so well known. If a truly great professor is fired for no reason, or no good reason, the market is there to scoop him or her up and make a better offer. Thus, arbitrary firings of great professors might be unsettling, and professors may not like an employment system where they are not bulletproof, but great professors will always have a home in a competitive industry or in the legal field.

So why is tenure so essential to these institutions? It is nothing more than job protection and a lifetime contract from under which an unhappy university can never get out.

The tenure reform proposal in this book is designed to attack this problem within the framework of reality. That reality is that most professors working now have tenure, and the universities have no means to change the terms of those grants even if they wanted to do so. However, universities can and should change employment terms and options for employees moving forward.

Universities can do so by preserving "traditional" tenure for the truly exceptional scholars, researchers, innovators, and grant producers whose reputation and economic value are set such that the lifetime offer is always a good value. At most universities, that is less than a handful of scholars.

In a world where we have freedom of contracting, we ought to let these institutions have the freedom to make a lifetime deal. However, we ought to set the bar much higher, so as not to confuse world-renowned experts and scholars with average professors, teaching in fields of study that ultimately have no bearing on the reputation or value of a university.

The problem with the tenure reform plan, of course, is that it requires buy-in by the education industry that created the existing system. It requires every institution to take the same revolutionary action, or to have a market leader make these changes and force other institutions to follow. Indeed, if that did not happen, professors would bleed out from institutions that don't offer traditional tenure and pour into those still willing and able to pay the freight.

In fact, some strategic game theory might have academic competitors stealing young talent and overpaying for them just to handcuff another institution. That's why voluntary academic and tenure reform of the type I discuss, can only come from market leaders such as Harvard, Yale, Stanford, Duke, and others. However, voluntary "reform," radical as it may be, is not the only method to reform tenure.

To fundamentally transform our colleges, cut costs, increase competition, lower student debt, and add intellectual diversity without voluntary leadership from a large swath of wealthy, prestigious universities, we must do something a bit more radical. At Mason Law, one can hardly take a class without hearing the correct economic and social mantra: Incentives matter. Indeed, they do.

What if Congress passed a law that prevented any government funds, research, or subsidized student loans to go to any institution in the country that doesn't adopt tenure reform policies meeting certain criteria? How radical would that be? Congress, obviously, can't tell public or private universities how to contract with their employees. But every single university in America except for Hillsdale College accepts federal funds in some form or capacity. What if the feds made tenure reforms a precondition to receiving federal funds of any kind?

Isn't that government interference? When government money is used, the government can make the conditions of the use or receipt of that money as it wishes.

That would be a revolution, and it would change the economic structure and incentives of higher education. Ironically, it would ultimately save the federal government billions, because eliminating tenure and moving to a contract-based employment system with mandatory retirement ages would dramatically cut university costs. Those dramatic cost savings would reduce the amount of federal dollars used to prop up institutions.

What would such a reform look like and how would it be implemented? First, it would necessarily require that existing tenured faculty be grandfathered. Likewise, because tenured faculty sometimes move and change jobs, both for personal necessity and to improve their professional standing, the grandfathering system would have to be portable. In short, those still in the system could remain in the system even if they changed jobs. This would immediately eliminate much of the pushback from existing faculties.

Make no mistake, nothing appeases an angry crowd more than an assurance that existing faculty have and keep their tenure rights. Of course, the federal government could also create a tenure buyout pool of grants that universities could apply for that would help them buy out the retirement of tenured professors. Once "retired" from any institution, such a professor would then be out of the grandfather system. If such a professor decided to go back to teaching, he or she would then enter the contract system.

A NEW TENURE AND CONTRACTING SYSTEM

1. To receive federal funds, universities may offer lifetime, traditional tenure to up to 2 percent of their total faculty body. This preserves tenure for the most elite and most valuable assets. It would also drive up compensation for that small, elite group. Universities may ask for an additional 1 percent waiver on the requirement, as needed. In addition, universities may buy and trade tenure rights up to 5 percent of the total faculty number. Thus, for cash considerations, an institution that wanted to get from 2 percent tenured to 5 percent tenured could buy tenure credit from an institution that does not have such a need or would prefer cash in hand and the ability to use the contract system.

2. It's critical to recognize that free contracting permits any institution that does not want any federal money to opt out of this system and retain its own free-market system where it continues to grant lifetime tenure to as many professors as it deems fit.

3. The contract system would have features that permit teaching contracts of no longer than 10 years. These contracts, from 1 to 10 years, would spell out and define academic freedom, and they would exclude from termination of the employment contract any activity related to that academic freedom. The industry would be encouraged to offer 1-, 3-, and 5-year terms originally in order to assess faculty productivity.

4. Contract offers would be done by a hiring committee of a university that includes an appointee of the university president, the department dean or his designee, two academic administrators, and two faculty members. This would be a "model" system, not mandatory. The concept would be that hires would reflect current and emerging goals of the institution and department, and not merely reflect the wants and desires of faculty to hire like-minded friends and scholars, as happens too often now.

5. New tenured faculty would have tenure expire at 60. Once it expired, they would then enter the contract term arrangement.

6. The terms, compensation, and conditions of any term-contract holder would be entirely between the employee and the entity. Thus, while a highly sought-after faculty member may not warrant tenure, he or she may warrant a host of terms, salaries, and conditions that each institution thinks serves its needs best to win the desired academic and retain them in the contract system.

7. States would be encouraged to permit "merit-based" pay, rather than "title-based" pay. This would permit universities to offer different salaries to employees within a range or class of titles based on merit, experience, and

value. That system would offer more flexibility, and it would eliminate the type of fake-title job engineering as described earlier in this book that encourages state entities and unscrupulous actors to create a legal fiction in order to fill a job or title.

8. Lifetime tenure could not be offered to any professor prior to 7 years of service in the contract system under the new guidelines.

These reforms would not all need to be part of a congressional plan. That is, smart universities willing to reform costs now could enact these changes on their own, though losing faculty to competitors unwilling to change is the risk. However, in many state systems, it is long overdue that tenure have an age cap on it at which time institutions are free from employment that sometimes becomes like a marriage, until death do they part.

Reducing overhead, being able to eliminate unnecessary positions, and being nimble enough to create and eliminate programs is essential for institutions to meet the needs of students in this global economy. It permits resources to be applied as and where needed, while capturing savings and attracting students on price and value. This includes attracting international students too.

Tenure reform is the best weapon to eliminate dubious majors, reallocate resources to much-needed majors and emerging fields, and dramatically reduce costs all at the same time. Tenure reform allows us to attack the largest costs a university has, which include the hard costs of lifetime labor and the immeasurable lost opportunity costs. In addition, deregulation of accrediting agencies will permit more adjunct faculty and allow all institutions to use more part-time industry experts, at cheaper costs. If you want to downsize higher education costs, you must restructure and downsize higher education overhead.

To save higher education and reduce debt, Americans need to return higher education to the mission of serving the best interests of the customer, rather than the pecuniary interest of the tenure class. We must reduce or eliminate the tenure tax.

Chapter 16

How Does a Student Find Value Right Now?

AN EXPERT AND FACT WITNESS

In the winter of 1990, I enrolled at Brookdale Community College in Lincroft, New Jersey. I was 23 years old, and I had zero college credits. The love and faith of a remarkable woman, now my wife, was a major impetus for my finally applying. She had already graduated college, as had so many of my friends from my high school graduating class of 1985. In 1989, I had a life-changing event that also set in motion my path back to higher education. It is from that experience that my journey from short-order cook to law dean and legal expert began.

I was in the office of the HR department for Monmouth County, New Jersey, then merely called "Personnel." I was hoping to find a solid county job. I had run for office at age 19, and I had helped to run two small businesses in my hometown. In my mind, I was a great candidate for a position of responsibility. To the hiring world, I was a high school graduate. That automatically eliminated virtually every job I would have wanted.

My meeting that day with an HR specialist named Joan was prearranged, and she explained to me that she had "pulled all the jobs for which I was qualified." She later explained why I was unqualified for the other jobs, and she nicely said to me, "You're a really smart guy; I think you should take the job with the highway department because you can be a supervisor in a few years."

The job paid about $17,000 a year. It came with an orange shirt and shovel to help get the dead animals off the road. She didn't tell me that, of course. I already knew that. I opted for a job with the Department of Weights and Measures as a "trainee," making $14,500 a year. I worked weekends at a pizza place to supplement my income. However, when I left that HR office

⠸BROOKDALE

UNIVERSITY PARTNERSHIPS

Figure 16.1.
https://www.brookdalecc.edu/regional-locations/university-partnerships/.

that fateful day, I knew for certain that I would never again sit in a room and have someone tell me all the jobs for which I was not qualified. Now, I had to figure out what to do about it.

I investigated the community college, and I found out that before I could even take a college course for credit, I had to take a remedial math class of high school level algebra. It was offered at 8 a.m. on Saturdays for four hours. That was the first college class I ever took, and it cost me $52 a credit. I spent much of that class wondering if any of this could ever, in any way, be worth it.

In late September of 2000, I made my way down to the HR department of my new job. There, I charmingly encountered the nice woman who ran my paperwork when I was hired. I sheepishly said to her, "Wow, this may sound funny, but I didn't get paid last Friday." She looked at me funny. She said, "You know, we only pay once a month." She explained it was all in my welcome package.

I let her know that I had not received such a package, but that I had read every company policy that week. She laughed, looked over at a stack of papers, and found a large envelope with my name on it. She said, "Well, if you didn't get this, then you also don't know that you got a raise too." I'd been working 2.5 weeks and got a raise. This place was great.

I opened the letter, looked at it, and then asked her, "Is this a prank?" She assured me it was not. I had an offer letter at home from my firm's hiring partner offering me a salary I never thought I would make in my life. It was $92,000. The letter in my hand from that envelope explained that during the three months between my previous offer and my coming to start the job, someone gave me a $33,000 raise. I didn't need algebra to do that math, but I sure needed that first remedial algebra class to put me on a path to that job.

I started my college career back at community college hoping to get an associate's degree and transfer to a state university. If the plan worked out, I would someday teach high school history and maybe help coach the baseball team. My plan got all jacked up, I like to say, and I wound up in law school. Joan in the Monmouth County HR was right, I was a pretty smart guy.

The smartest decision I ever made was to invest in myself. The second smartest decision I ever made was to do it as cheaply as possible. In fact, I paid for my associate's degree by working three jobs and living at home until I was married a few years later. I borrowed as little as necessary to get through my last two years at the state college, Rutgers.

When I graduated Rutgers, I was still working at the Department of Weights and Measures, and I was making $25,000 a year. Now, with a degree, I was considering law school. Only because of my low debt did I decide to apply for that advanced degree. In fact, at a dinner celebrating my graduation from Rutgers, my mother asked me how I was ever going to pay back all those law school loans I was considering borrowing. I told her, "Mom, I can borrow $30,000, and when I get out, the average salary of a graduate is $56,000. It will work out!" It did.

I was lucky. Let's put a sharp punctuation on that. Yes, I worked hard. Yes, I had a measure of academic success. I also had the struggles and doubts of any returning student. Mostly, however, I was lucky that school was dramatically cheaper years ago, and even more lucky that I was so grossly unqualified to attend any other institution that I was forced to go to community college. It was dirt cheap, and it was the exact right place for a kid like me to start and reenter the academic world.

Likewise, I went to law school when the market was down, and I graduated when it was up. I attended a great school, and the tuition was remarkably cheap. It turns out that the seventh child of blue-collar parents can't help but look for value, since money he does not have.

The rest of my story is in these pages previously. I worked at a major law firm. I left there to work in the cybertechnology world, ultimately becoming the CEO of a company. When we sold that company, I returned to my law school to be an administrator and teacher. In between, I ran for office, worked with my alumni group, had children, and ultimately got to coach baseball too. Now I am back practicing law. All those events, however, were made possible by investing in additional skills that were useful in a job market.

The first realization I had in returning to school was that simply having skills, connections, or talent is not enough. In this world, the market demands that someone validate those talents, and that is done through the degree process. Joan in HR didn't have anything against me. She couldn't hire me for the jobs I wanted because they required a degree. In fact, that baseline requirement of a degree has become a minimum standard for most jobs.

Certain trades can still be quite profitable, but those jobs require different skills and strengths than I possess. I have a brother who is an amazing carpenter. He can not only see designs in his head, but he can draw them and bring them to life. That has seemingly always been cooler than anything I have ever done. My brother never went to college, and it is likely his money would have been wasted there. Likewise, if I had spent the last 20 years on the set of *This Old House*, I probably still couldn't hammer a nail in with three strikes.

Life has a strange way of revealing to you all the things you can't do. Indeed, my list is seemingly longer than most. I sometimes joke that no one is less capable than me. If life would have more easily revealed to me what I could do, I might have started working at it much earlier.

Finding our skill set and a marketplace for those skills is a lifelong endeavor. Indeed, education is in every way a daily event for those who recognize that once we stop learning we have already begun to die. Accruing useful knowledge, experience, and the wisdom of lessons learned is an essential part of maturity and happiness. Only a very small part of this education process is our formal training and education. But it is critical as a building block to our economic success. Finding, developing, and investing in the skills we need to live does require some risk, but it should not require catastrophic debt. We must find value.

Our national obsession with getting a degree stems from the idea that all education is equal. As we discussed, it is not. All education has a value, but some skills are valued more in the market. Likewise, some of the valuable skills we need in the market can be obtained far more cheaply than others.

In seeking skills for the marketplace, we need to seek relevant skills, applicable to our strengths, at a cost that best positions us to leverage those skills. Ideally, finding value initially will put us in a position, if appropriate, to acquire even more skills through an advanced degree.

THE VALUE OPTION: COMMUNITY COLLEGE

I believe community colleges remain the best, untapped resource for the American educational consumer. Community colleges focus on job skills, retraining, and relaunching students. The schools provide valuable skills at a steep discount. More importantly, for the older student, the unsure student, and the struggling student, they provide a platform more amenable to success. They likewise provide a platform where failure and risk do not amount to a lifetime of debt.

When I reentered the world of education, I did so with great fears of failure. I did so begrudgingly, and I did so without much confidence. Likewise,

I approached community college as if going there reflected poorly on me. In my very narrow mind, community college was for people not good enough to go to real college. Many there, like me, were not ready for "real" college, whatever that was.

What I quickly learned at my community college is that I was there because that is exactly where I belonged at the time. Now, I look at community college as a remarkable gateway for many students. It is the perfect place for all students not headed to the most elite institutions. Indeed, why would any student who must pay for his or her own education start anywhere else unless the student is on scholarship?

If you look at the advertisement for my fair old Brookdale Community College (figure 16.1), it smartly advertises that it has partnerships with many New Jersey universities. Those partnerships are the same in most states. One can take one's AA (associate's degree) and apply those credits, in whole, to a four-year degree. That means half of your education is at a dramatic discount on tuition. For those attending community college, most of whom already live at home, it is also a savings on room and board. It's a savings on travel and gas. It's a savings on nearly every aspect of your noneducational costs.

One of the reasons why community college is such a great value is because those institutions often do not use tenured faculty and lifetime appointments. Even those that do, have lower salaries and a singular focus on teaching. There is no appreciable tenure tax.

If you are neither a scholarship student nor a student for whom someone else is paying the entire cost of a four-year college, community college is the first place to look to build your academic career. If it turns out that you can't cut it, then you have lost less money. If it turns out you have picked a major or field about which you change your mind, you can course-correct without a major loss of investment. It is a lower-pressure entry point at a significantly lower price point.

Students and parents obsessed with attending a four-year college, networking, or having the "college" experience are often overvaluing those considerations. If you are not attending an elite university, or a regional powerhouse steeped in tradition with a strong alumni base, you are paying for hype, not networking. Worse than that, you are paying for tenure, social services, and hand-holding. You are paying for buildings and infrastructure, all of which will not get you a valuable degree at a lower price.

Minimize your debt footprint by taking as many classes as you can at a community college. Make sure you understand all the state programs and transfer rules. As discussed in an earlier chapter, students may qualify to attend community colleges free based on a host of criteria. In addition, under some state programs, they may also transfer and receive a discount on state university tuitions to fill out their four-year degree.

Here's the other outstanding feature of attending most community colleges. When you transfer, the institution takes your credits and you graduate with a degree from the four-year institution. You get all the leverage of a Rutgers degree, for example, even with only two of your four years in attendance at that institution. I keep my community college experience on my résumé. I feel it is a badge of honor. I likewise like that it helps to tell the story that I was ready to relaunch and restart at an older age, and unafraid to do to whatever I had to in order to build that academic credential.

STATE UNIVERSITIES

If you are determined to spend four years at a college, then do it at a state university. To be sure, some of the best universities in this country are state schools. In fact, that is because states wisely invested in colleges years ago to have an educated population. In addition, they invest in those institutions to steal the population of other states and attract the best and brightest from one state into their own.

States recognize that upon graduation most people who came from another state for college will ultimately stay in the state, settle, find work, and become a productive taxpayer. That's a great form of economic development. In addition, state universities are an excellent place for elite students who fall short of getting into the most elite private schools.

Some state institutions, like the University of Virginia, or Cal Berkeley, for example, are enormous academic powerhouses. As a result of their reputational status they can be as hard to obtain admission from as nearly any other elite institution. Likewise, they are getting expensive, and they have all the structural liberalism problems discussed herein. However, they are state subsidized. That means, your parents have been paying your tuition ever since they paid any taxes in your state. While they may seem like a better bargain, the truth is, residents have already merely prepaid some tuition. If the kids go there, they then obtain the benefit of that subsidy or prepayment.

Even at state universities, one must consider not merely price, but value. Is the school of sufficient reputational rank? How do its graduates do in the field in which one may want to study? Many parents take their kids on school visits, which are carefully organized propaganda tours. That's fine. Anyone looking to move to and live at a university ought to tour the facility and get the feel of it. They ought to do that repeatedly, and certainly educational consumers should seek out more than just in a guided tour where university officials put on their best face. Tour it, talk to students, and find alumni.

This book is not meant to supplant the innumerable tools and resources one *must use* and study to compare academic institutions, majors, employment prospects, and debt management. When a person decides to invest in anything, including himself—especially himself—due diligence and research are required.

For example, you may want to study business at a state college. That's great. How does the college rank for business? How do its graduates do in getting real jobs in the business world? You don't want to see stats and numbers about business majors generally, you want to see the numbers from that institution specifically. You want to talk to the graduates, and any decent undergraduate institution should have a list of graduates in any program that you can call to discuss the graduates' experiences while there. When you do that, see if you can get other contacts from that graduate not on the "school's list." If you are going to spend tens of thousands of dollars on an institution, you should spend countless hours doing your research before that investment.

If you are going to a state university because you insist that you must do so rather than first attending a community college, or you legitimately find the community college in your area will not prepare you for your field of study, then consider attending the institution as a commuter. This assumes doing so saves you time and money.

There is a theme here, and it is simple. You want to obtain the best, most usable educational degree at the cheapest price, and from the best institution you can. One of the primary reasons for this principle is to have available to you additional money for additional education if that too becomes a wise investment. Saving money early on will permit you to obtain an advanced degree or additional training and certifications in your field. If you don't continue on in higher education, saving money lets you to invest in a business, a home, or other items essential to your happiness.

Acquiring a degree must be about value over simple cost, or worse yet, over the failed notion that you must have any degree, no matter the cost. Here is a college value checklist. It's simple, and we start from the premise that you do not have a college fund or funder, or that your ability to obtain academic scholarships is limited. It further assumes that you have demonstrated the ability to attend college and the requisite maturity to thrive there.

THE VALUE CHECKLIST

1. Cost and reputation. What are the total costs of the school and how is its generic reputation in the community and regional job market?
2. How old is the institution, and how heavily involved are its alumni?

3. What resources does it put into placement, and what opportunities does it offer for solid connections for both internships and externships in *your field of study*?

4. What do employers think of the institution, and do many major employers recruit there or have partnerships with the school?

5. Is recruiting in your field at that institution growing?

6. How active are the alumni in student life and job placement?

7. What are the teaching ratios, and does the school narrowly focus on several strengths for which it is known, or is it like a New Jersey diner offering numerous suspect choices?

8. Does the institution have a large endowment, and does it use that endowment to invest in scholarships for students, clinics for practical experience, or business partnerships for placement?

9. Does the institution have flexible, part-time options to which you can readily change if you need time to work or earn money?

10. What is the total cost of the education? That is, does a higher cost of living, commute, or hidden fees drive up your overall costs?

11. How responsive, efficient, and helpful are the staff? If they are not great to prospects, they will not be improving once the institution hooks you.

12. Assuming cost and expertise are similar, how well does this institution rank in the county, state, region, or even nationally? How portable is that degree?

13. How recent, specific, and useful are the employment numbers, salary data, and job placement? Any school unwilling to discuss these in detail is suspect. Any school that merely uses platitudes or generalizations, or refers you to a webpage only, is a cross-off.

14. If this is a state school, are there programs to achieve testing out of certain requirements? Will they accept other credits, such that you can transfer existing community college credits, or obtain such community college credits to supplement your course work if easier, cheaper, and more convenient?

15. Are the atmosphere and physical environment safe and conducive to learning and cooperation?

Ultimately, you are trying to marry cost and reputation to obtain value. Many years ago, I developed a very simple formula—maybe it is more accurately described as a slogan. It goes like this.

If you can't go to Harvard, Yale, or Stanford, go to the best state college you can attend. To that I now add, study the most useful major, at the lowest price, at the best institution into which you can gain admission. And when in doubt, get every credit you can at the lowest cost.

Unlike the book's earlier example, don't live in New Jersey and obtain an English degree from another state's school. That is literally wasting your money. If you must do that, move to that state first, obtain domiciliary status, and apply later as a state resident. The year you spend getting residency and working will dramatically cut the costs of being out of state for four full years.

If you are entering higher education in the next few years, no reforms will have changed the reality of the structural liberalism this book discusses. Accordingly, until the revolution, you must be both a bargain and value hunter. Revenue predators are real. Cronyism is real. The tenure tax is real—and structural liberalism, it is a leviathan. You can't solve those problems, but awareness can help you find a value education until the revolutionaries can rebuild this broken, dysfunctional, self-serving system.

Good luck, and as I once told my law class in a graduation speech, don't forget to be awesome.

Epilogue

My take on higher education is radical. The truth sometimes is the most radical concept of all. Because of the structure and unique take on higher education in this book, I asked a diverse group of individuals to read the book and provide me feedback. Some wanted a deeper dive of statistics. Some wanted fewer, less specific examples. The consensus, however, was that the book focused on the right approach to identifying the problems and offering solutions.

The biggest problems and issues in this country are hard to fix because "solutions" cause pain to large numbers of people who are doing fine without those solutions. In addition, many of our most complex problems are not merely a function of policy, but a reality of our culture. The great debate over the Second Amendment, as some see it, or guns, as others see it, is a prime, relevant example. Mass shootings, a subject on which I have written and researched significantly, reflect all the issues and problems we face when attacking a real problem with innumerable contributing causes, the roots of which are cultural.

Higher education has a culture problem, and we are part of it. We all want to be educated. For parents, all we want is for our kids to succeed, and where possible excel and surpass our expectations. For most parents, those expectations are already quite high for our kids. It is easy to buy into the arguments that more money and more resources make for better education in the K–12 ages and that a large investment in college is essential once a student graduates. Spending money only helps in education or life if it is spent and invested wisely.

Our culture has replaced the value aspect of education with the false, cultural liberalism premise that all higher education is good without regard to value. This book challenges that assumption, both with the research it cites, the numbers it quotes, and the specific, albeit anecdotal, examples I share.

Let's talk about some of these examples. First, any good scholar will tell you that anecdotal examples are not the basis for policy change. That is true. They are only powerful and useful if the data likewise show a significant problem and the examples help bring that data to life.

No one can contest that the cost of higher education is a problem. No one can contest the growing and catastrophic size of student debt. No one can contest the growing size of institutions, faculty, administrators, and costly amenities at expensive and often mediocre schools.

My examples demonstrate how that happens, but they don't purport to say that every institution has a cronyism problem. If my test readers, a psychologist, an author, a judge, and an elementary school educator, had a common theme of criticism, it was that my examples identifying specific problems in one institution felt too personal. I took that criticism to heart, and I greatly narrowed the details to reflect the needs of the book. The book is not meant to be an indictment of any single institution or person. However, it would be incorrect to assume or forgive conduct that generates the very costs and problems on which the book is focused.

Make no mistake, there are much more personal, difficult, revealing, and troubling tales to tell about a handful of characters, but this book and this time are not the place for them. To the extent the examples used trouble you, the more troubling part of the examples should be the reality that in a country with thousands of colleges and universities, it is more likely than not that these types of problems are prevalent and driving costs and debt.

Since leaving my role at Mason Law, I am back practicing law, still appearing on radio and TV as an expert on legal and political issues. Likewise, I launched a blog that examines legal, political, and higher education issues. In a little over a year, the site has amassed over 1.5 million views on subjects simple and complex. The book notes some of the articles related to higher education. I invite you to visit the site and see the conservative perspective on those issues, as well as legal and political issues of the day.

I would direct you to three pieces that examine higher education, the role of revenue predators, and the system's troubling move away from critical thought. They include "The Left's War on Thinking," "If the *US News* Law School Ranking Is the Bible ... It Needs a New Testament," and "Harvard Law, the LSAT, the ABA, the Tenure Tax, and Revenue Predators."

I sometimes create short videos as well, and the one titled "Think" remains a popular video. A former law professor of mine inspired it. These pieces I mention, collectively, were the inspiration for compiling my thoughts, research, analysis, and experiences on higher education to create this book, which I hope you find valuable.

Glossary

The book introduces some new terms and concepts. It also uses other familiar terms in a new setting. Accordingly, it might be useful to define some of these terms and place them in context to help the reader.

Structural Liberalism: Higher education has created a web of policies, regulations, procedures, accepted practices, methods, and operational systems that, taken together, create a unique structure that forms the whole of our educational system. Structural liberalism is the sum, while other components of that sum include additional defined terms, including "cultural liberalism" and "political liberalism."

Cultural Liberalism: This phenomenon is a political, social, and economic set of principles that disconnect market theory and efficiency from higher education as a good, service, or product. Sometimes it is used interchangeably with "political liberalism," but in reality, cultural liberalism is a by-product of the effects of political liberalism as those effects have been incorporated into our greater society. Some examples might include more safety nets, more social programs, and a laxer, less demanding society. There is less independence as young adults, and more dependence on government and family and a growing expectation of entitlement and help.

Political Liberalism: The term is a hobgoblin. Modern liberal politics is many things, but it is not classic, Western liberalism as once studied and advocated by Western thinkers and libertarians alike. Modern, American, political liberalism as used in this book reflects the more hard-left, alt-left, big government, redistributionist view that has come to take root in the

American left. It is marked by resistance to social norms, a predisposition to outrageous behavior, and a marked movement away from civil disobedience and intellectualism. Political liberalism is marked by anger, emotion, classism, identity politics, and perverted ideas of social justice.

Alt-left or Alt-leftism: This is the American hard-left movements. Decades ago, these were pure socialists or communist sympathizers. Today, it is the more violence-prone, openly defiant, pro-fascist side of the left, often marked or typified by entities or groups using fascist tactics and techniques in the name of anti-fascism.

The Dubious Degree: This is the face of social justice and alt-leftism as reflected on higher education degrees in nonmainstream topics and subjects. These aren't merely soft-science or Western-leaning humanities and liberal arts degrees that help to build writing and critical thinking skills, these are degrees in radicalism, disconnected totally from market skills and needs and designed to create social justice warriors.

Tenure Tax: This represents the cost of providing instructional services over and above the market price of such services. The tenure tax is in the cost of lifetime employment, inefficiency, and low productivity, which drive instructional costs through the roof.

Revenue Predator: This is an undistinguished college or university with easy admission, low endowment, and numerous dubious majors and programs designed to lure students in primarily for revenue rather than for the good of the student.

Notes

CHAPTER 1

1. The 2016–2017 tuition, room, board, and fees for Harvard, without any financial aid, was $63,025. Of course, this value assumes two factors, neither of which is likely to be true. The first is that a student won't qualify for some form of grant or aid, and the tuition won't increase for four straight years.

2. The Cowboys should have won that game, but alas they were robbed when Deion Sanders was not flagged for pass interference.

CHAPTER 2

1. In the law school world, *US News and World Report* creates a gold-standard ranking system used by educational consumers. The institutions loathe it, all of whom still work to game the system to increase their relative ranking. Generally speaking, it breaks schools into tiers, and first-tier schools are in the top 50. The power of the rankings is not in its flawed, often easily manipulated methodology. The power is in its market force, where prospective students treat the ranks as a lost gospel, certain that school 41 really is better than school 43.

2. *The Docket* went on to apply market principles after its budget was cut by student government due to prior years' poor performance. The paper raised all its own revenue, published biweekly, and ultimately was honored with a national newspaper award from the ABA law student division.

CHAPTER 3

1. George Mason raised its undergraduate tuition 5.5 percent for the fall of 2017, charging $5,862 in just tuition, per semester, for full-time undergraduate students taking 12 to 16 credits. https://studentaccounts.gmu.edu/wp-content/uploads/Fall2017Undergraduate.pdf.

2. These are a few of the very many, innumerable majors offered at George Mason University. https://advising.gmu.edu/current-student/majors-at-mason/.

3. Strong beginning salaries in enduring careers are always tied to proven, lasting industries that require real, market-based skills. This *Forbes* piece looks at the top-20 starting salaries by major, collected from data used by Glassdoor. https://www.forbes.com/sites/jeffkauflin/2016/10/17/the-20-college-majors-with-the-highest-starting-salaries/#158125fa2d50.

4. http://www.nadaguides.com/Classic-Cars/1982/Dodge/Aries/2-Door-Sedan/Values.

5. http://www.nadaguides.com/Classic-Cars/1982/Porsche/911-Targa/2-Door-Coupe/Values.

CHAPTER 4

1. Not surprisingly, healthcare costs are also rising because of liberalism and a complex, multipayer, highly regulated system that reduces efficiency, mandates coverages, sets price floors, and manipulates the markets. See my piece explaining health insurance at www.committedconservative.com (the direct link is here).

2. The newly appointed dean did find a cost to cut. It was that assistant dean, whom he later replaced with two hires at nearly four times the cost, in a subject carried in my chapter on cronyism.

CHAPTER 5

1. This is an example of the incorrect view that deans control universities. They may grow like weeds there, but they are subject to extermination, unlike the army of tenured professors with lifetime employment. See the essay "Who Runs the Colleges—Administrators or Faculty?" by Ronald Lipsman at https://www.mindingthecampus.org/2013/04/who_runs_our_colleges-_admini/.

2. Term faculty or contract faculty are teachers or professors who are not tenure-line. They might be great professors, impressively credentialed, and well qualified in their field, but they are not scholars or researchers of the right pedigree or philosophy, so schools hire them on a contract basis to fill a specific need that is not covered by tenured faculty.

3. The carbolic smoke machine case stands for the proposition that declarations by advertisers who state that a product is the best, or tastes the best, are opinion rather

than fact. As such, they do not create an enforceable contract on which a consumer may rely, if he or she buys the product and finds it not to be "the best." The declarations are said to be "sales puffery."

CHAPTER 6

1. An informative though incomplete analysis of the phenomenon was published in a piece at the *Huffington Post*, citing numerous research sources. http://www.huffingtonpost.com/2014/02/06/higher-ed-administrators-growth_n_4738584.html.

2. George Mason University once ran a campaign with posters that showed a condom and a banana. Posters aren't free, and neither are the people who think up such campaigns. Isolated, these costs might be minor. Aggregated, they add to your tuition bill.

3. A March 2, 2015, article and survey on college administrators' salaries can be found at Inside Higher Ed. https://www.insidehighered.com/news/2015/03/02/study-finds-gains-college-administrators-salaries.

4. See the illuminating article on college spending at the Forbes.com website. https://www.forbes.com/sites/caranewlon/2014/07/31/the-college-amenities-arms-race/#3f333ad84883.

5. Idem.

6. Idem.

CHAPTER 7

1. Each of the test readers had comments about this section, and the book has seen a redraft from its first several iterations of this chapter. These anecdotes are not intended to distract from the broader analysis of this book. One Mason Law student read the book and liked it very much, but ultimately, he was concerned it had the feel of sour grapes and would be so portrayed. No doubt, it is 100 percent correct that it will be portrayed that way. However, the story of Serfs and Lords cannot be told in theory, it must be detailed with real facts. These facts give life to a complex, pervasive, and costly problem that is often not even on the radar of most writers and thinkers. That the book identifies some individuals whose actions and conduct impacted the author is the reality of life experience. That they provide a teachable moment for the readership is the primary purpose of inclusion.

2. One tenured faculty member appointed to the dean search committee exclaimed at a search committee meeting that "no one else in the country is qualified to be the dean of George Mason Law." That is transparently untrue. Indeed, any of the finalists, and several of those who applied and were not finalists, could have competently run Mason Law.

3. Butler asked me to stay on, removing me from administration, but creating a new director of the Mason Law Community title. Ultimately, it was designed to ease me out the door without having to immediately fire me as soon as he came on board.

4. Dean Manne wanted to control the Mason Law Review and reshape, in his mind, its quality and direction. The Law Review refused. Manne set up a second Law Review in the law school. Ultimately, they were merged in a reconciliation.

5. Butler also was forced to scramble and offer a pay increase to stop another possible high-level departure during the early part of his rocky tenure as dean.

CHAPTER 8

1. Dr. Stearns retired as provost but remains, of course, in the tenured faculty. His page reads, "Dr. Stearns retired as Provost in June 2014 but maintains a robust faculty schedule. He has published widely in modern social history, including the history of emotions, and in world history; and has authored or edited over 135 books, mainly in social history and world history. From 1967 to 2016 he served as editor-in-chief of *The Journal of Social History*" (https://historyarthistory.gmu.edu/people/pstearns). Dr. Stearns, according to public records, made $290,845 in 2016 as a professor (http://data.richmond.com/salaries/2016/state/george-mason-university).

2. The George Mason University sports name is the "Patriots," and the university president likes to address communications to employee and alumni by leading with "Dear Patriots."

3. The court held that FOIA requests, by their statutory definition, cannot reach the foundation, irrespective of how close the relationship is with the university, or how many people seem to play dual roles. In the end, the foundation is not a state agency, and is thus not subject to the FOIA. You can read the court's order here: https://www.opengovva.org/transparent-gmu-v-george-mason-university-order.

4. After the announcement of the gifts became public, there was political caterwauling on campus and nationally. The grant agreement setting out the terms of the gift was leaked, and that leak led to a lengthy discussion about the real intent and purpose of the gift. Many left-leaning university professors focused on the intention of the donors to, in their view, wrongly and politically influence higher education. Few, if any, focused on the long-term cost of the deal. The grant agreement, which I reference in this chapter, can be found here: http://www.gmu.edu/resources/facstaff/senate/Countersigned%20GMU%20-%20CKF.pdf.

5. Subsequent to writing this chapter, and before publication, news broke publicly questioning George Mason's fundraising agreements dating back to the early 2000s. The university president issued a statement admitting that some agreements ceded academic considerations to donors. President Cabrera exempted himself and this agreement from that criticism, though in reality, the donors purchased a strong position on the law faculty.

6. Certainly no one who reads this book thinks it is my intention to defend Henry Butler. However, being self-serving doesn't mean every decision he makes is without merit.

CHAPTER 9

1. See September 20, 2017, *US News* article on schools with top endowments: https://www.usnews.com/education/best-colleges/the-short-list-college/articles/2017-09-28/10-universities-with-the-biggest-endowments.
2. http://colleges.startclass.com/l/4437/University-of-Virginia-Main-Campus
3. http://colleges.startclass.com/l/4362/Christopher-Newport-University
4. http://colleges.startclass.com/l/4375/George-Mason-University
5. http://gmufourthestate.com/2014/03/09/masons-endowment-funds-pale-in-comparison-to-other-virginia-colleges/.

CHAPTER 10

1. This from a website and company that will gladly profit off you by consolidating your existing loans with them. God Bless America. https://studentloanhero.com/student-loan-debt-statistics/.
2. https://www.cnbc.com/2017/08/29/student-loan-balances-jump-nearly-150-percent-in-a-decade.html.
3. https://www.becker.edu/academics/undergrad/division-of-humanities/global-citizenship.
4. https://fivethirtyeight.blogs.nytimes.com/2010/09/19/consumer-spending-and-the-economy/.

CHAPTER 11

1. You can't make this stuff up. http://themarkromano.com/index.php/2017/08/29/racism-professor-uses-classroom-to-shame-white-students/.
2. http://foreignpolicy.com/2017/08/17/donald-trump-is-a-nazi-sympathizer/amp/.

CHAPTER 13

1. I have been a part of two of these reaccreditation exercises. The first time I was a member of my law school alumni board, and the second time I was on the other side as a law school administrator.
2. At the political and legal website I founded, www.committedconservative.com, I have written a substantial 3,000-word essay on the legal rankings, how they work, how they are manipulated, and how law schools work to game them. I also offered substantial reforms that while not perfect, would dramatically improve the accuracy and value of those rankings. The piece is titled "If US NEWS Law School Ranking Is the Bible . . . It Needs a New Testament."

Notes

CHAPTER 14

1. From a 2013 NPR story on college majors. http://www.npr.org/sections/money/2013/09/10/219372252/the-most-and-least-lucrative-college-majors-in-1-graph.

CHAPTER 15

1. I was that assistant dean. The story is included here as a snippet because of its relevance to the discussion of the need for tenure reform. No intelligent discussion of tenure reform can take place without acknowledgment that the purpose of tenure, and its protections, is designed to combat real abuses in the system. The entire story of this episode can be found at www.committedconservative. com. The title of the story is "Abuse of Power: The Day the Virginia Attorney General Tried to Get Me Fired." http://committedconservative.com/2017/11/03/abuse-power-day-virginia-attorney-general-tried-get-fired/.

About the Author

Richard Kelsey is a trial lawyer in Virginia and the founder and editor-in-chief of the conservative legal and political website www.committedconservative. com. Kelsey has appeared as a legal expert and political commentator on radio, TV, and in print hundreds of times. His appearances include Fox Business News with both Charlie Payne and Neil Cavuto. Kelsey also provided the legal analysis of Virginia Governor Bob McDonnell's corruption case for the DC affiliate of NPR. He still appears regularly on Virginia Public Radio as a legal expert. His writing can also be found at *The American Spectator* and CNSNEWS.com.

Kelsey is a former assistant law school dean and former technology CEO. At George Mason Law, he served as the alumni president and was the inspiration for and creator of its Center for the Protection of Intellectual Property. In addition to his administrative duties as the assistant dean for management and planning, Kelsey taught law and was chosen by the class of 2014 as its faculty speaker at graduation.

Kelsey lives in Virginia with his wife Jill and their three kids. On most weekends, he can be found coaching, umpiring, or rooting for his sons at a local baseball field.